Editor
Eric Migliaccio
Jennifer Overend Prior, M. Ed.

Managing Editor
Ina Massler Levin, M.A.

Editor-in-Chief
Sharon Coan, M.S. Ed.

Illustrator
Kelly McMahon

Cover Artist
Barb Lorseyedi

Art Coordinator
Kevin Barnes

Imaging
Rosa C. See

Product Manager
Phil Garcia

Publishers
Rachelle Cracchiolo, M.S. Ed.
Mary Dupuy Smith, M.S. Ed.

Math Centers

Author

Traci Ferguson Geiser, M.A.

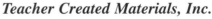

Teacher Created Materials, Inc.
6421 Industry Way
Westminster, CA 92683
www.teachercreated.com
ISBN-0-7439-3718-X
©2003 Teacher Created Materials, Inc.
Reprinted, 2003
Made in U.S.A.

Table of Contents

Table of Contents *(cont.)*

Introduction

The Early Childhood Centers series was created especially for busy teachers of young children. The hands-on, developmentally appropriate activities are sure to provide your students with hours of fun-filled learning experiences throughout the year. The activities are set up in an easy-to-follow format and require little preparation time and few materials. Each center is designed to reinforce skills typically taught in early childhood programs. The Skills Reference Chart on pages 8 and 9 will guide you as you blend the activities with your existing curriculum.

Early Childhood Math Centers provides young children opportunities to practice math skills that will prepare them for higher-level math learning. Each chapter offers several different activities to reinforce math skills. The centers in each chapter vary in level of difficulty, as well, and address different learning styles in order to meet the individual needs of your students.

The chapters will focus on the following skills:

- **Counting:** The centers in this chapter focus on recognizing numerals and counting up to the number fifteen. Children will have opportunities to use one-to-one correspondence while participating in fun hands-on games and activities. Activities range from the simple to the complex to help you meet the needs of each of your students.

- **Patterns:** Patterning is the building block for many math concepts. Children who have had experiences creating and extending patterns are able to more easily grasp many math concepts. Activities in this chapter will give your students the opportunity to identify, create, and extend simple and complex patterns. You can simplify each activity by using only one or two pattern sequences (for example, AB, ABC, AAB). As children become more comfortable with patterning, they will identify and incorporate patterns in their daily activities.

Introduction (cont.)

- **Sorting and Classifying:** Activities in this chapter will give children practice sorting and classifying in an exciting, child-friendly way. Some centers focus on sorting objects by just one characteristic, while others give children the opportunity to sort by more than one characteristic. Your students are sure to be challenged and feel successful, regardless of their level of ability.

- **Shapes:** Children will enjoy activities in this chapter focused on matching, drawing, and identifying basic shapes. Distinguishing the differences in basic shapes and learning the shapes' names are important early geometry skills.

- **Sequencing:** The centers in this chapter help children to identify and sequence events, letters, numbers, and patterns. While students perform these activities, they will also gain practice in left-to-right correspondence and problem solving.

- **Measurement:** Children will enjoy using a ruler as they begin simple measuring tasks. This chapter gives children various experiences with comparing shapes and sizes as well as measuring objects. Complete with a measuring stick for each student, these centers provide the perfect activities to introduce young children to the concept of measuring.

- **Graphing:** This chapter will give your students hands-on opportunities to explore graphs. Children will learn how to interpret data from graphs and transfer data to graphs. They will also create their own graphs through the center activities. Written especially with young children in mind, this simple first look at graphs is a great head start for little mathematicians.

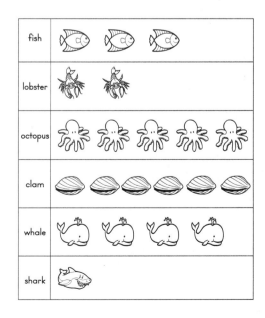

Introduction *(cont.)*

What Is a Center?

A center activity is designed to give children individual or small group practice in developing skills. The activities are usually easy for children to accomplish with little or no assistance from the teacher. While students work on independent center activities, the teacher is free to work with a child or small group of children without interruption.

The Early Childhood Centers series was designed with young learners in mind. It features developmentally appropriate, hands-on activities to engage and hold the attention of young children.

Why Use Centers?

Center activities provide children opportunities to learn how to work independently while learning essential skills. Most centers feature methods for student self-checking that enable children to check their work and, if necessary, problem solve to find the correct answer.

Children working in small groups during center time can teach each other valuable skills and information through their work together. Group problem solving can lead to meaningful discoveries that can have a lasting effect on learning.

Center Assembly and Organization

At the beginning of each center activity, a Teacher Preparation section informs you of what needs to be done before the center is presented to the class. The Materials section provides you with a list of all the materials the children will need in order to complete the center. Unless otherwise specified, you will need to make only one copy of each designated reproducible. You may also choose to color and laminate the centers for visual appeal and durability. Puzzle pieces should be cut carefully, making sure to cut around the tab pieces. If you wish to use the puzzles simply for matching you may cut the tabs off.

Prior to center time, it is important to thoroughly explain each center so every child has a clear understanding of what he or she is expected to do. The Student Directions section of each center gives clear step-by-step instructions for completing the center activity. The first day of a center rotation will require a little extra time to explain each center. On subsequent days, children who have completed a center can help describe the center activity to their classmates.

Introduction (cont.)

Always include a discussion of where and how the center materials are to be cleaned up and stored. Envelopes and plastic baggies are wonderful organizational materials. Label each envelope or baggie and the accompanying game pieces with matching stickers to indicate where each set of game pieces are to be stored. This will help keep materials organized and enable children to clean up materials easily. Small shoeboxes or trays may be helpful for storing center materials when they are not in use.

How Do I Manage Centers?

Center activities are best used when they are a part of the daily routine. A twenty- to thirty-minute block of the day is ample time for conducting learning centers. During this time, children may be put in small groups by the teacher and assigned names (red group, blue group etc.). The groups may rotate each day until each group has had the opportunity to complete each center. A simple color chart with clothespins (see the illustration below) helps manage this rotation.

If you prefer a less structured use of centers, you may wish to allow your students to choose the centers where they would like to work. In this case, you may want to limit the number of children in each center to be sure you have adequate supplies for each child to complete his or her task.

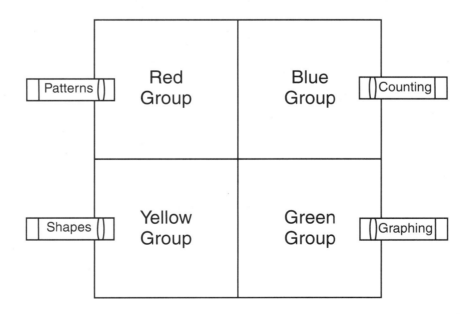

Skills Reference Chart

Skill \ Activity	"All Aboard!"	"Chocolate Factory"	"Candle Count"	"Complete the Caterpillar"	"Fishy Fun"	"Button Up"	"Cool Creations"	"Pasta Patterns"	"Nifty Necklaces"	"Keep On Truckin'"	"Flower Fun"	"Pattern Sort"	"Farm Animal Fun"	"Backwards Bingo"	"Book Bonanza"	"Zany Zebras"	"Shoe Sort"	"Class Sort"	"Shape Puzzles"	"Start Your Engines"	"In Shape!"
Matching Numbers to Sets	✔	✔																			
Number Sequencing	✔			✔																	
Counting			✔	✔	✔																
Recognizing Numbers					✔																
Writing Numbers					✔																
Creating Patterns							✔														
Extending Patterns							✔		✔	✔	✔										
Identifying Patterns												✔									
Sorting/Classifying													✔	✔	✔	✔	✔	✔			
Fine Motor Development						✔													✔		
Recognizing Shapes																			✔		✔
Matching Shapes																				✔	✔
Matching Shapes by Size																					✔

Skills Reference Chart *(cont.)*

Skill \\ Activity	"Shapes Everywhere"	"Cookie Time"	"Trace the Tracks"	"Fly Away Numbers"	"The Circle of Life"	"Beach Ball Alphabet"	"Fun With Food"	"Rhyme Time"	"Easy as 1, 2, 3"	"Measure Me"	"Growing Garden"	"Inch Worms"	"3 Bears Math"	"Hair Cut"	"Big Fruit, Little Fruit"	"Create A Graph"	"My Graph"	"Critter Count"	"Count on Me"	"Pie Graph"	"Pet Parade"
Number Sequencing				✔																	
Extending Patterns							✔														
Matching Shapes	✔	✔																			
Matching Shapes by Size																					
Drawing Shapes			✔																		
Fine Motor Development	✔		✔																		
Sequencing Events					✔			✔	✔												
Alphabet Sequencing						✔															
Measuring										✔	✔	✔		✔	✔						
Comparing Sizes														✔	✔						
Estimating Sizes												✔									
Creating Graphs																✔	✔	✔		✔	✔
Interpreting Data from Graphs																			✔		
Pie Graphs																				✔	

All Aboard!

Skill: Matching Numerals 1–10 to Sets, Number Sequencing

Materials: scissors; train cars (pages 11–13); number cards (page 13); pencil

Teacher Preparation: Cut out the train cars and number cards. Color and laminate train cars, if desired. Write the correct number on the back of each train car for student self-checking.

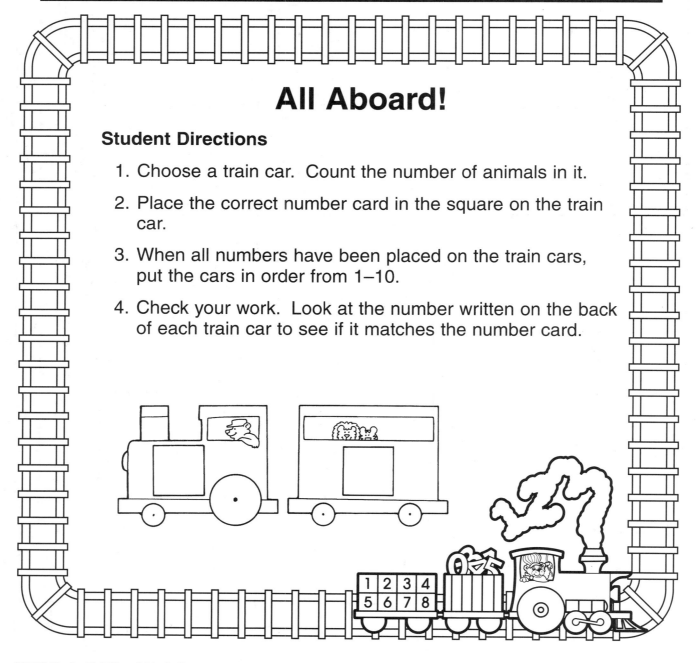

All Aboard!

Student Directions

1. Choose a train car. Count the number of animals in it.

2. Place the correct number card in the square on the train car.

3. When all numbers have been placed on the train cars, put the cars in order from 1–10.

4. Check your work. Look at the number written on the back of each train car to see if it matches the number card.

All Aboard! *(cont.)*

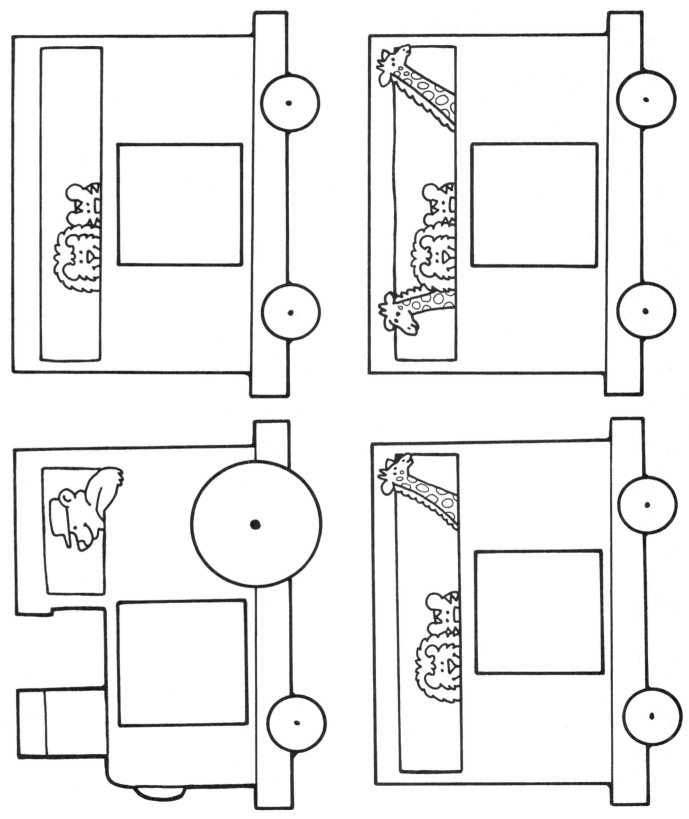

All Aboard! *(cont.)*

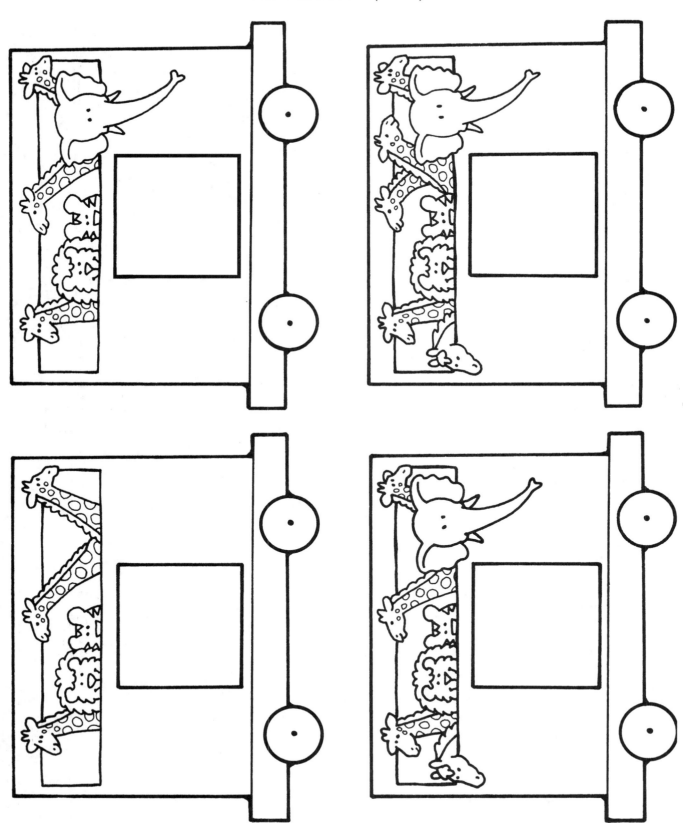

All Aboard! *(cont.)*

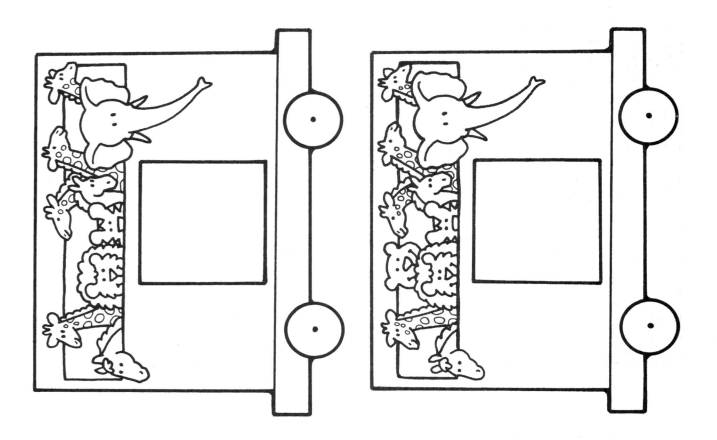

1	2	3	4	5
6	7	8	9	10

Chocolate Factory

Skill: Matching Numerals 1–10 to Sets

Materials: scissors; number boxes (pages 15–18); candy boxes (pages 19–20); pencil

Teacher Preparation: Cut out the number boxes and candy boxes. Color and laminate the number boxes and candy boxes, if desired. Write the correct number on the back of each candy box for student self-checking.

Chocolate Factory

Student Directions

1. Choose a candy box and count the pieces of candy in the box.

2. Put the candy box in the correct number box.

3. Continue until all candy boxes have been matched with the correct number boxes.

4. Check your work. Look at the number written on the back of each candy box to see if it matches the number on the number box.

Chocolate Factory *(cont.)*

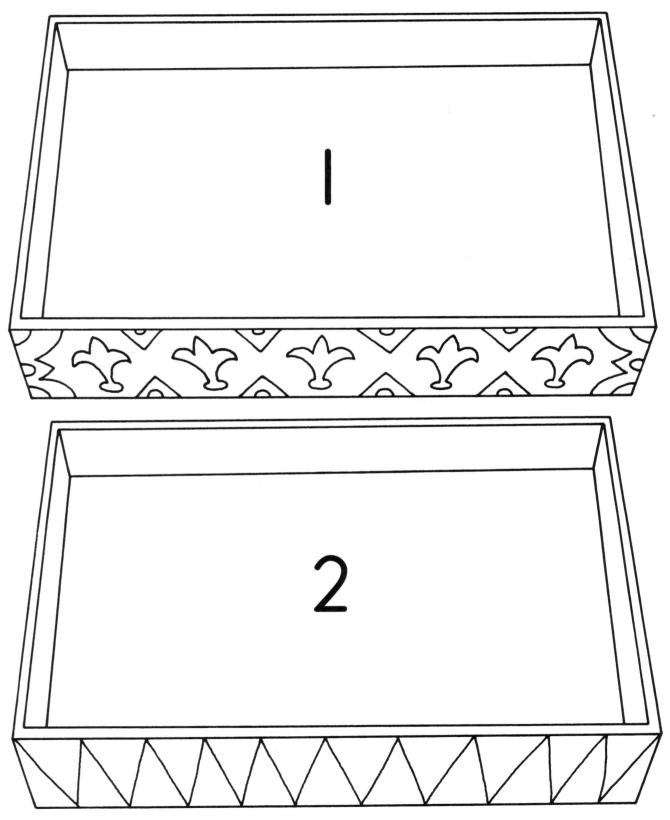

Chocolate Factory *(cont.)*

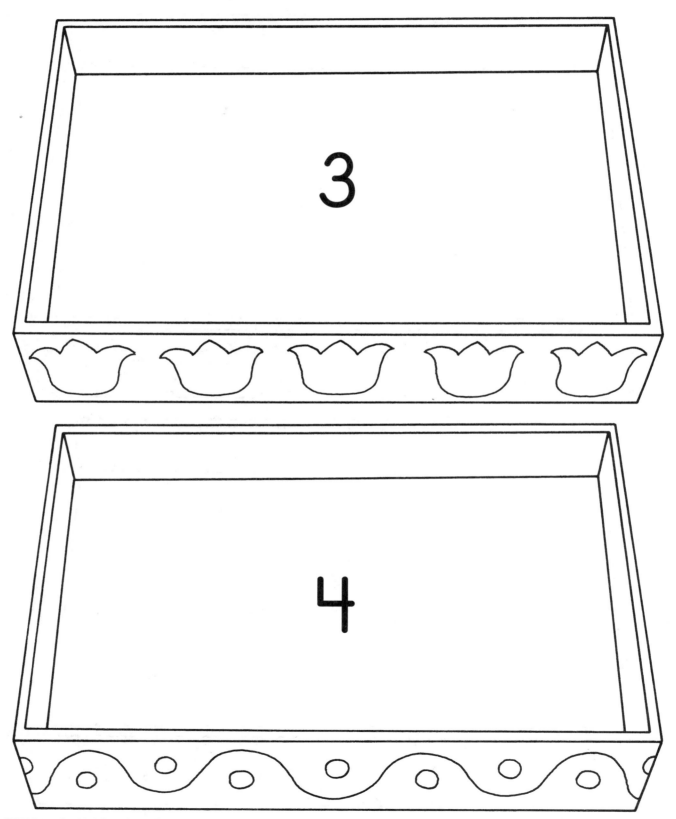

Chocolate Factory *(cont.)*

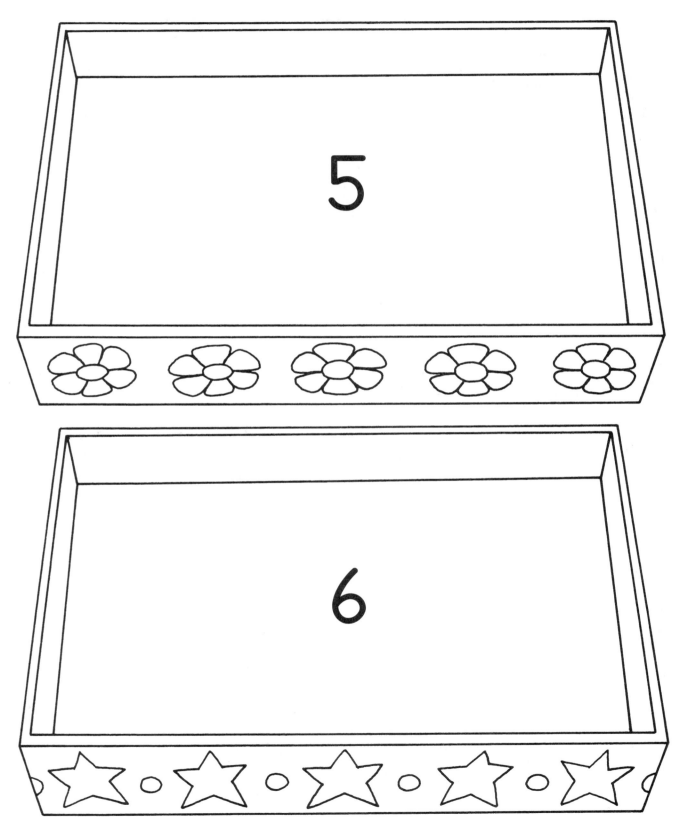

Chocolate Factory *(cont.)*

18

Chocolate Factory *(cont.)*

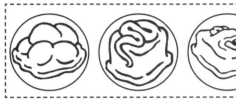  

Chocolate Factory *(cont.)*

Candle Count

Skill: Counting 1–8

Materials: scissors; cakes (pages 22–25); candles reproducible (page 26)

Teacher Preparation: Reproduce candles several times. Cut out cakes and candles. Color and laminate cakes and candles, if desired.

Candle Count

Student Directions

1. Choose a cake and read the number on it.

2. Place the correct number of candles on the cake.

3. Choose another cake and repeat the process until all cakes have candles on them.

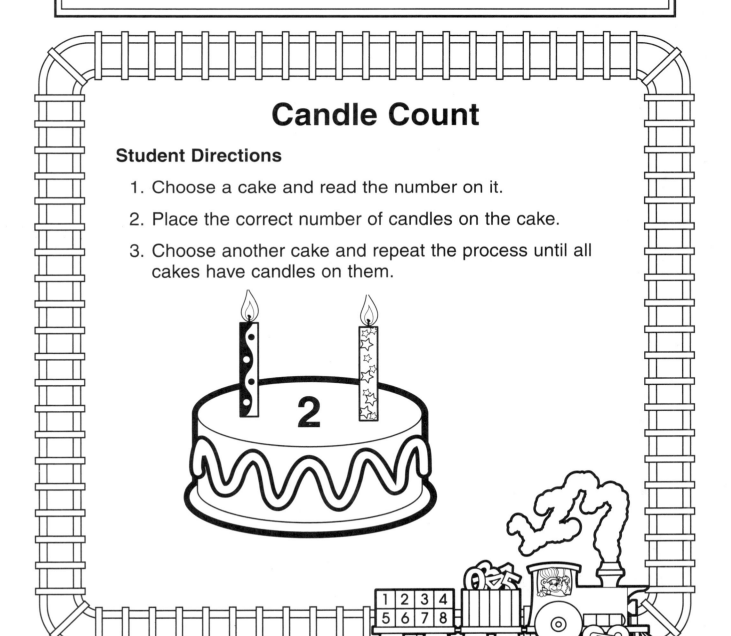

Candle Count *(cont.)*

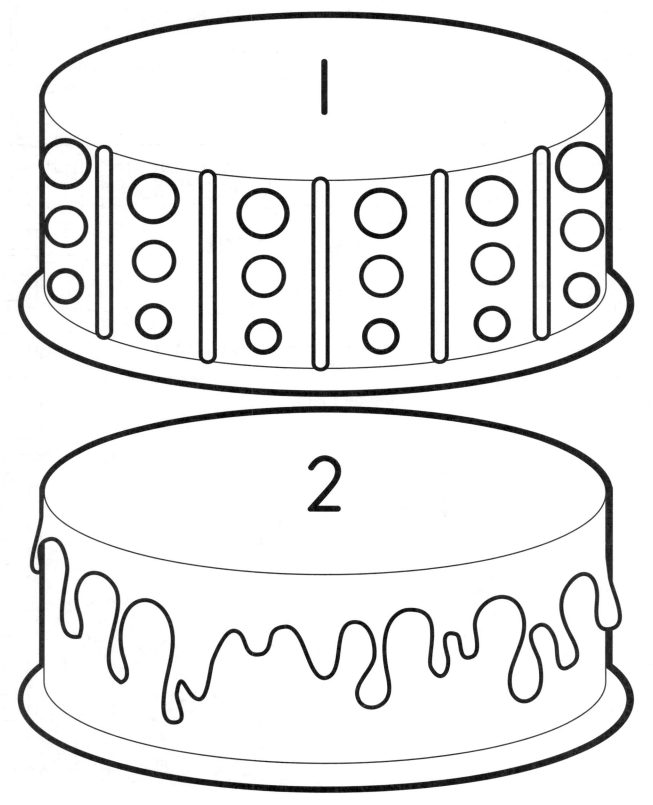

Candle Count *(cont.)*

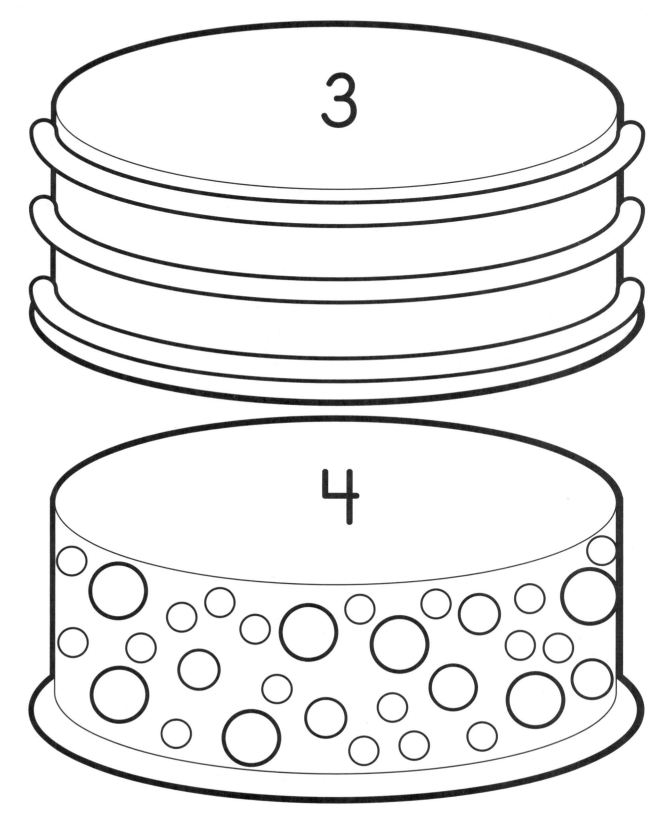

Candle Count *(cont.)*

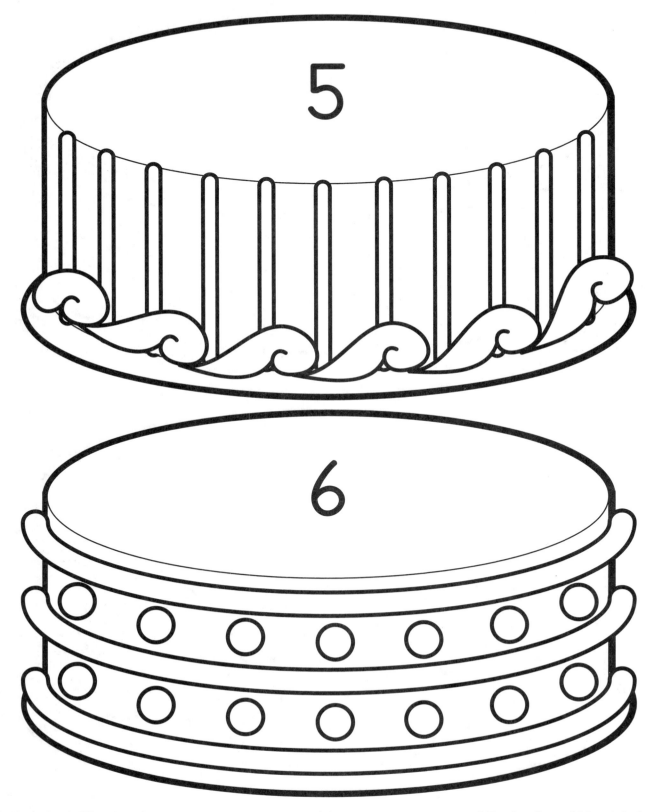

Candle Count *(cont.)*

Candle Count (cont.)

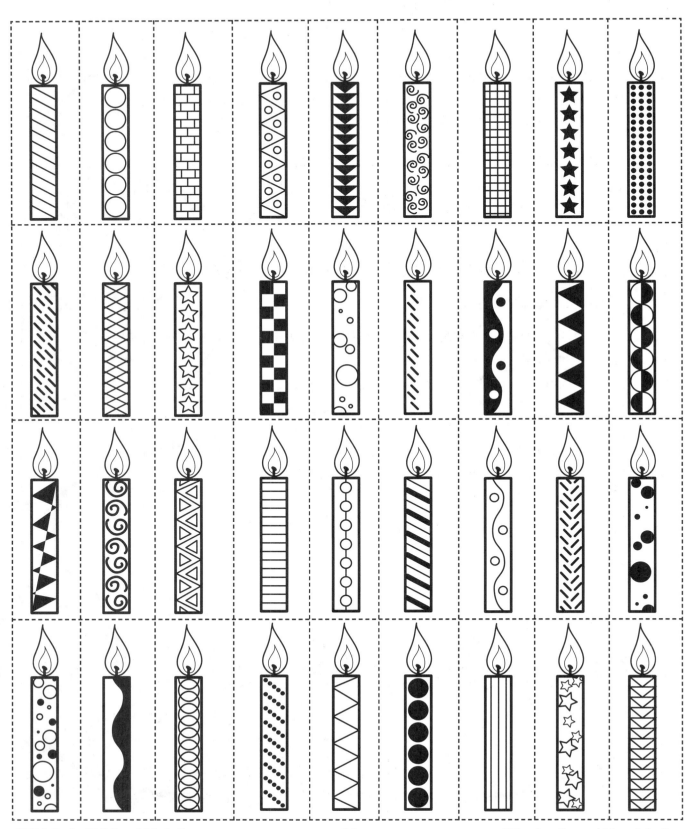

Complete the Caterpillar

Skill: Number Sequencing 1–15, Counting 1–15

Materials: scissors; caterpillars (pages 28–30); numbers (page 31); pencil

Teacher Preparation: Reproduce the numbers several times. Cut out the caterpillars and numbers. Draw the correct number of dots on the back of each number for student self-checking.

Complete the Caterpillar

Student Directions

1. Choose a caterpillar. Say the numbers written in each circle.

2. Fill in the missing numbers with the number cards.

3. Count the dots if you need help.

4. Check your work. Look at the back of each number and count the dots to see if they match the number of dots on the caterpillar.

5. Remove the number cards and choose another caterpillar.

Complete the Caterpillar *(cont.)*

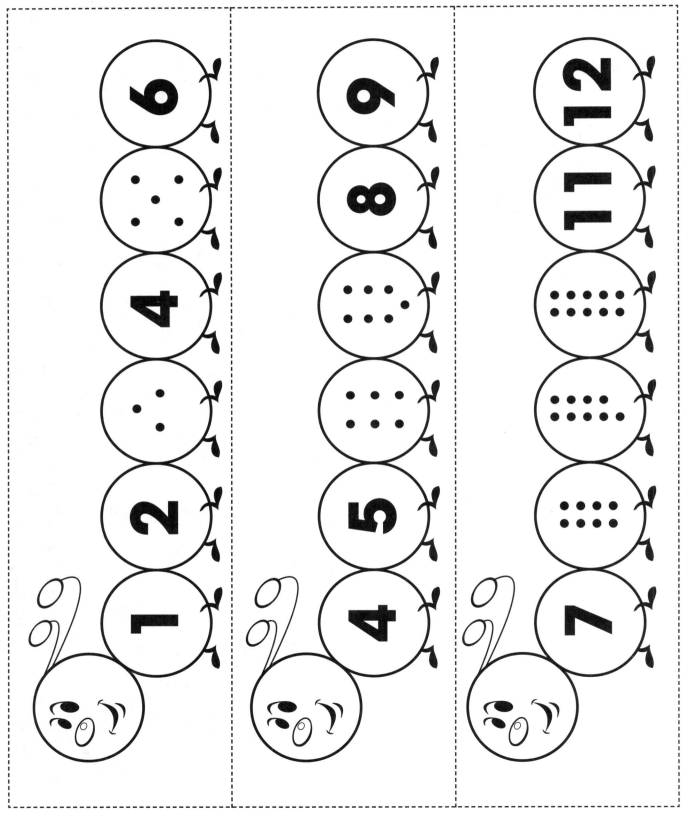

28

Complete the Caterpillar *(cont.)*

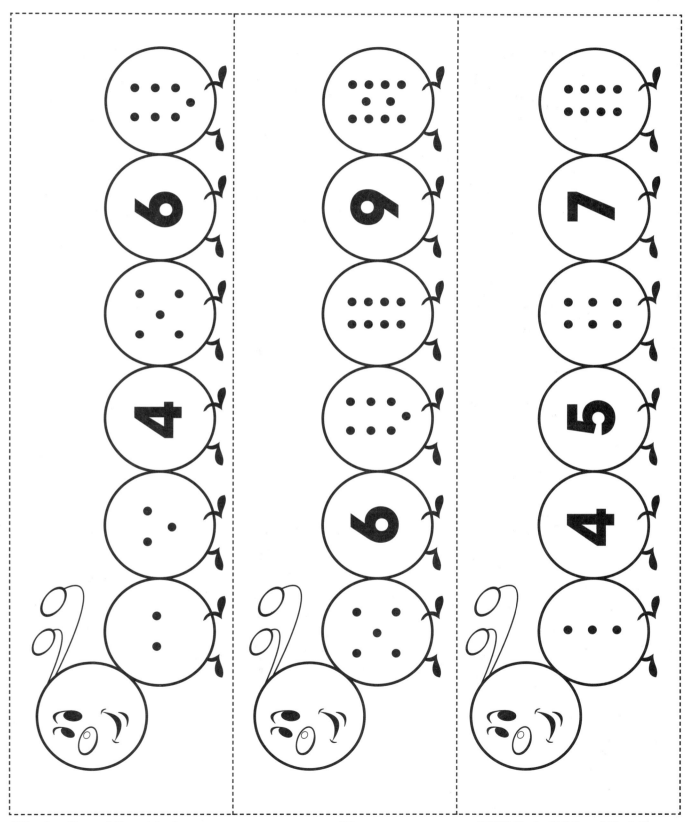

Complete the Caterpillar *(cont.)*

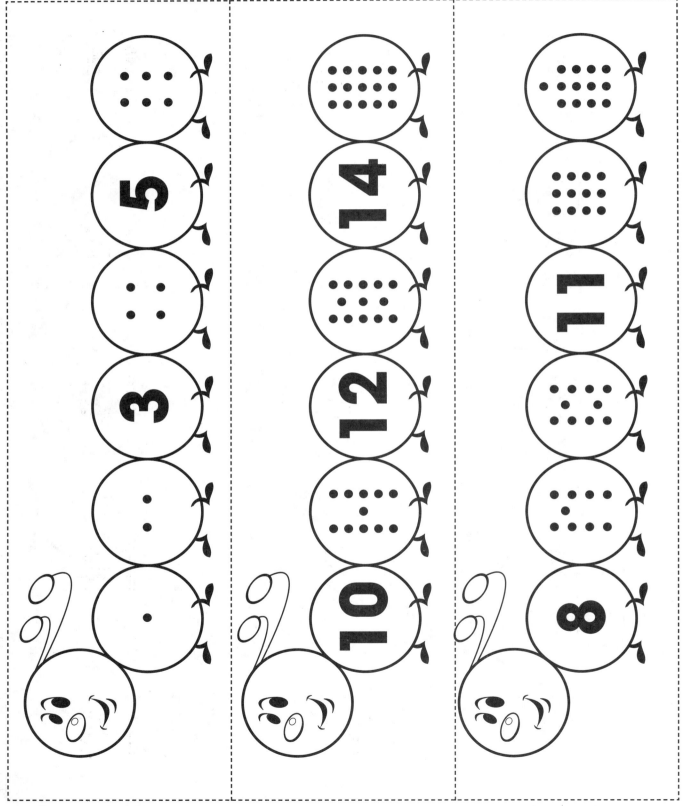

Complete the Caterpillar *(cont.)*

1	6	11
2	7	12
3	8	13
4	9	14
5	10	15

Fishy Fun

Skill: Recognizing Numbers 1–6, Writing Numbers 1–6

Materials: Fishy Fun mini-book (pages 33–36); fish (page 37); one die; pencils or crayons; glue

Teacher Preparation: Reproduce and assemble a Fishy Fun mini book for each student. Introduce the mini book by reading it and discussing each type of fish home.

Fishy Fun

Student Directions

1. Write your name on the cover of your book.

2. Turn to page one. Roll the die to see how many fish to add to the page.

3. Write the number in the blank at the bottom of the page. Use the helping page, if necessary.

4. Glue the correct number of fish cutouts to the page.

5. Repeat the process until the book is complete; then read the book

Fishy Fun *(cont.)*

Fishing Fun

A Counting Book

By _____

I see _____ fish in the fish bowl.

Fishy Fun *(cont.)*

I see _____ fish in the lake. ②

I see _____ fish in the river. ③

Fishy Fun *(cont.)*

4

I see _____ fish in the ocean.

5

I see _____ fish in the aquarium.

Fishy Fun *(cont.)*

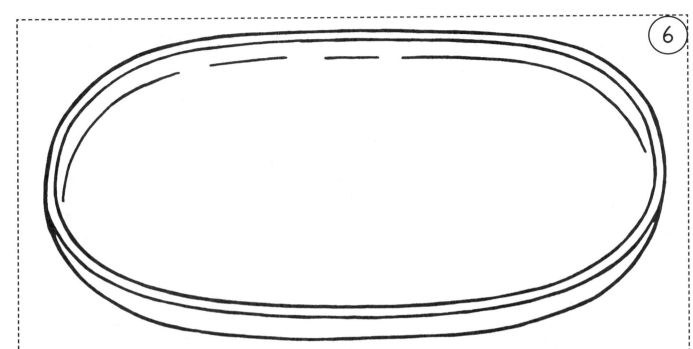

⑥

I see _____ fish on my plate.

⑦

Helping Page

⚀	1	⚃	4
⚁	2	⚄	5
⚂	3	⚅	6

Fishy Fun *(cont.)*

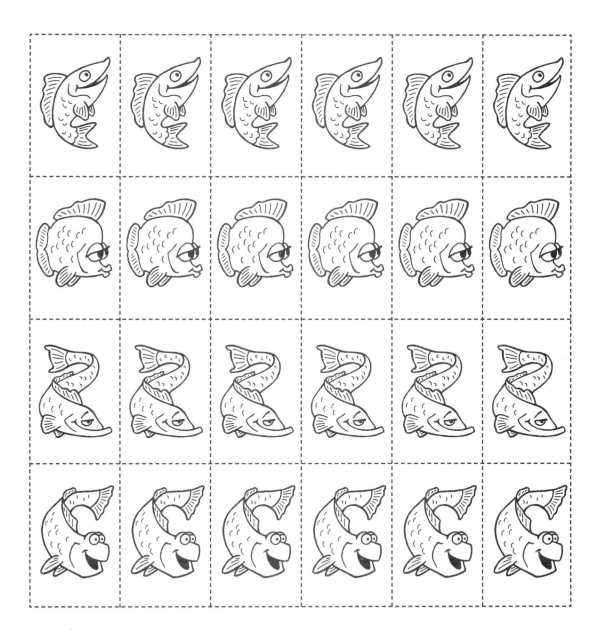

Button Up

Skill: Counting 1–10, Fine Motor Development

Materials: scissors; clothes and buttons (pages 39–42)

Teacher Preparation: Cut out clothes and buttons. Color and laminate clothes and buttons, if desired.

Button Up

Student Directions

1. Choose an article of clothing. Look at the number on it.

2. Say the number and count the same number of buttons.

3. Add the buttons to the clothes by placing one on each buttonhole.

4. Remove the buttons and repeat the process with another article of clothing.

5. On the coat with no buttons, draw as many buttons on it as you'd like on the coat.

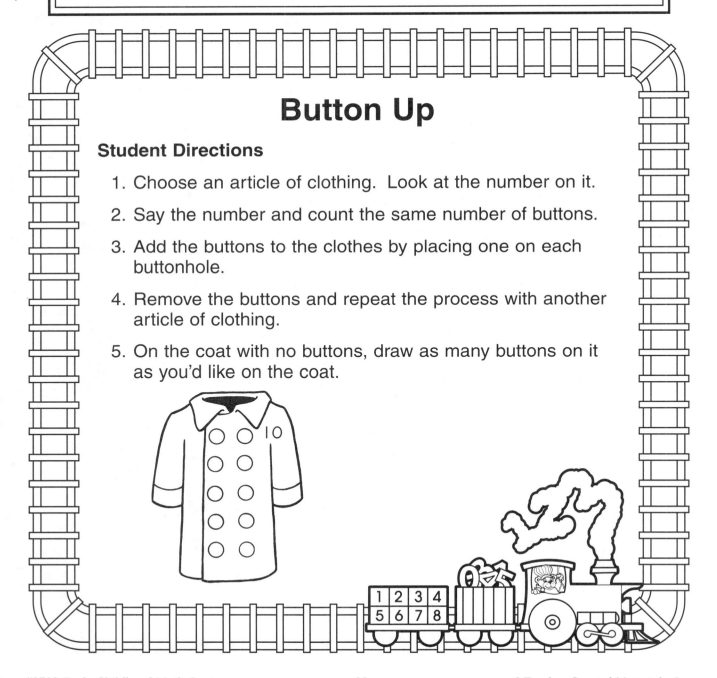

Button Up *(cont.)*

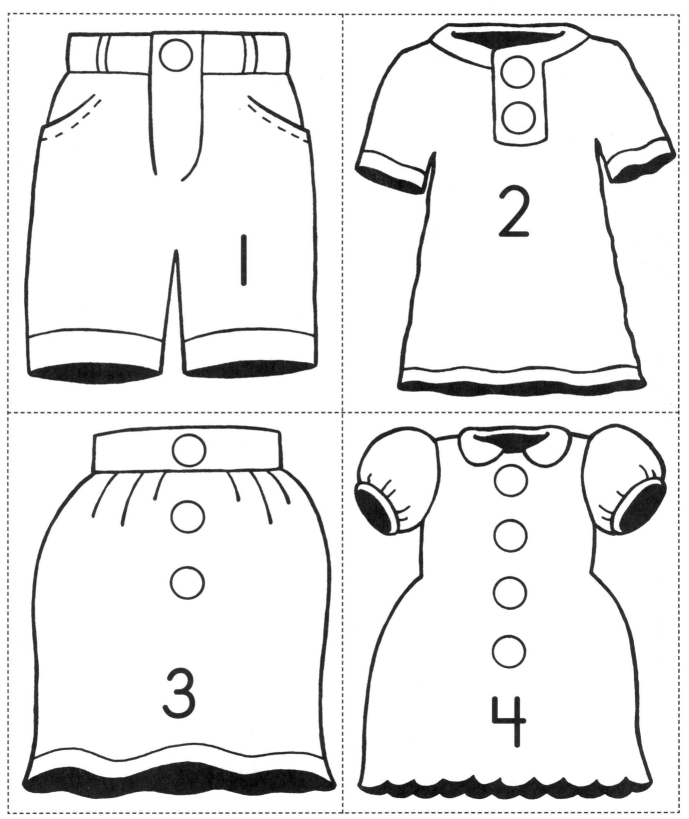

Button Up *(cont.)*

Button Up *(cont.)*

Button Up *(cont.)*

42

Cool Creations

Skill: Extending AB, ABB and ABC Patterns.

Materials: scissors; cones (pages 44–46); ice-cream scoops (page 47)

Teacher Preparation: Reproduce scoops several times and cut them out. Cut out the cones on the dotted lines. Color the cones and scoops as indicated on the key (page 47). Laminate the cones and scoops, if desired.

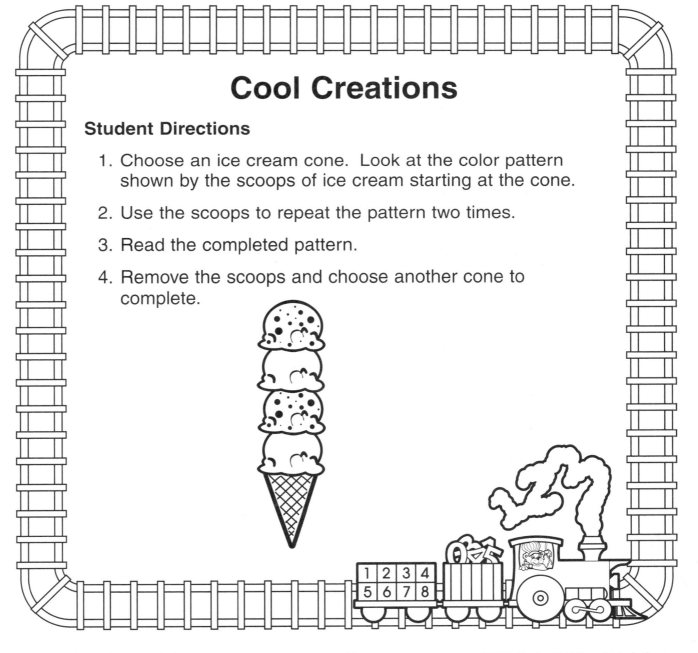

Cool Creations

Student Directions

1. Choose an ice cream cone. Look at the color pattern shown by the scoops of ice cream starting at the cone.

2. Use the scoops to repeat the pattern two times.

3. Read the completed pattern.

4. Remove the scoops and choose another cone to complete.

Cool Creations *(cont.)*

44

Cool Creations *(cont.)*

Cool Creations *(cont.)*

Cool Creations *(cont.)*

Key

 = white   = brown   = green   = pink

Pasta Patterns

Skill: Creating AB, AAB, ABB, and ABC Patterns.

Materials: pattern cards (pages 49–52); scissors; pasta (page 53)

Teacher Preparation: Cut out pasta. Laminate pattern cards and pasta, if desired.

Pasta Patterns

Student Directions

1. Choose a pattern card.

2. Choose a different kind of pasta for each letter at the top of the card, and then put the pasta in the corresponding box.

3. Starting at the arrow, look at the pattern at the bottom of the page and replace each letter with the correct piece of pasta.

4. Remove the pasta pieces and find a new pattern card to complete.

Pasta Patterns *(cont.)*

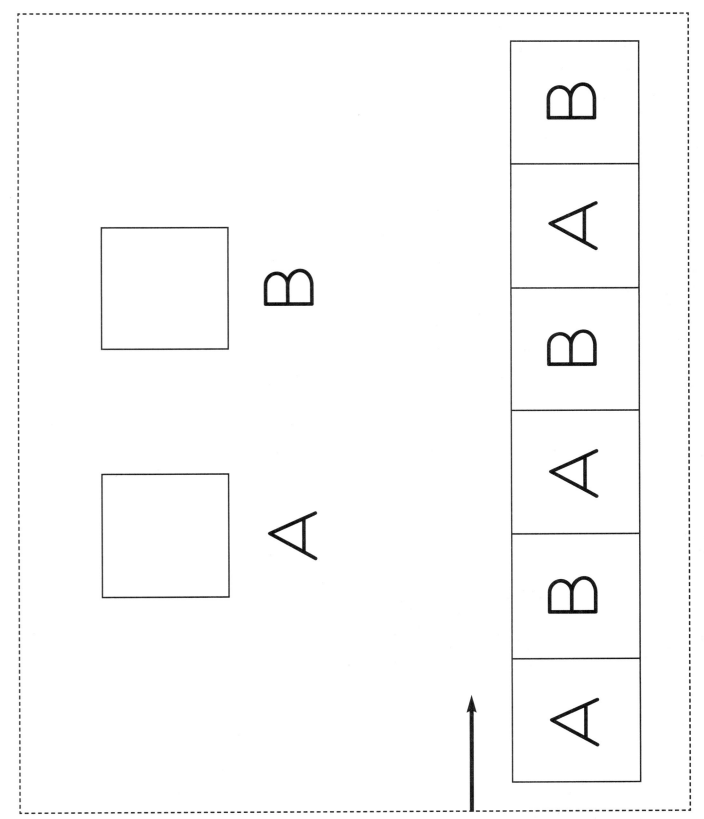

Pasta Patterns *(cont.)*

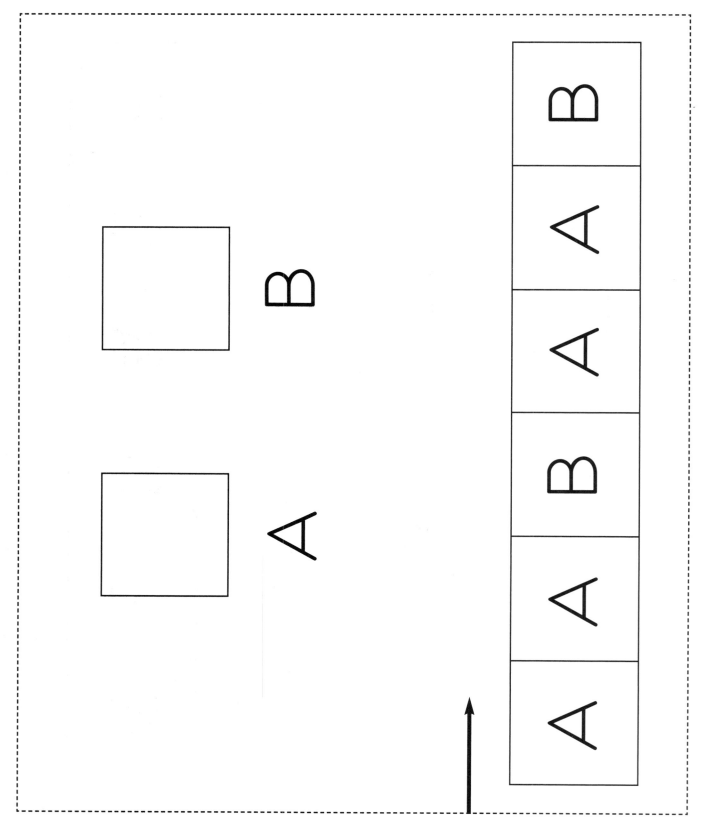

50

Pasta Patterns *(cont.)*

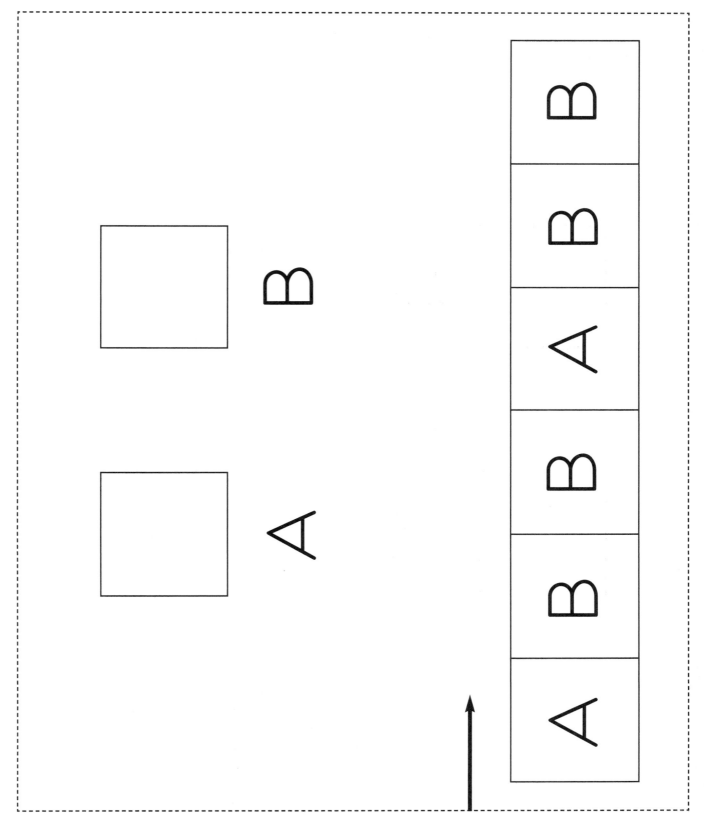

Pasta Patterns *(cont.)*

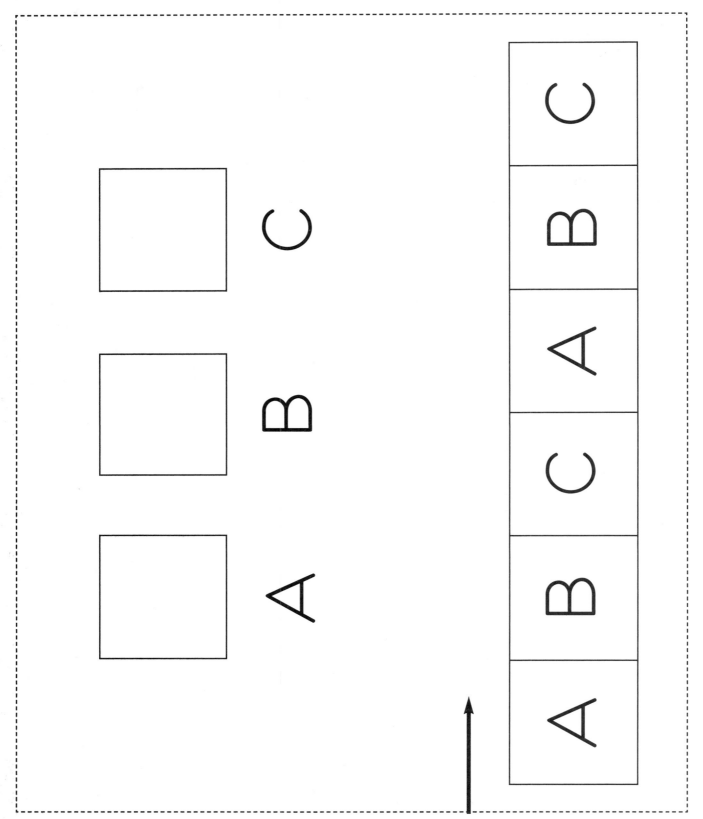

52

Pasta Patterns *(cont.)*

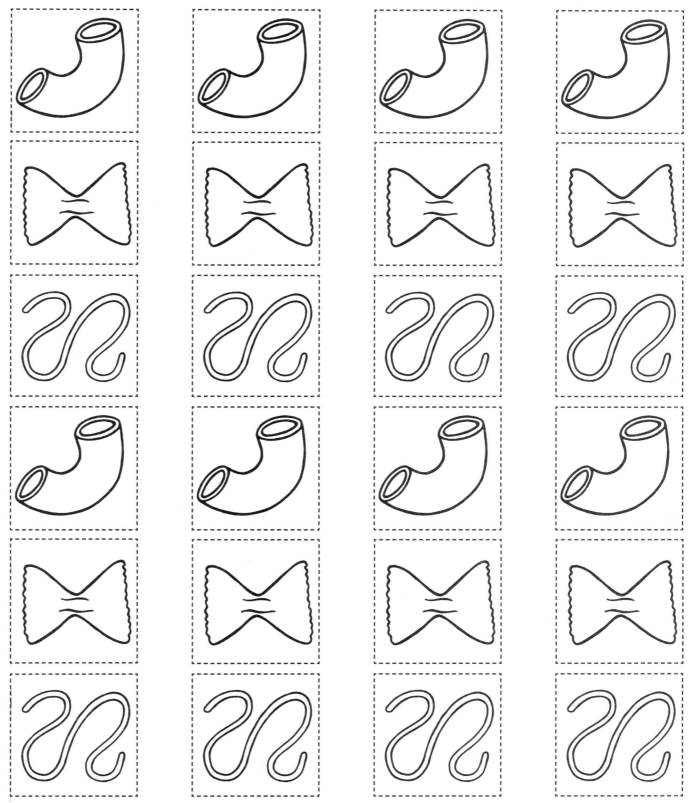

Nifty Necklaces

Skill: Extending AB, ABB and ABC Patterns.

Materials: scissors; necklaces (pages 55–57); beads (page 58)

Teacher Preparation: Cut out beads and necklaces on the dotted lines. Color and laminate beads and necklaces, if desired.

Nifty Necklaces

Student Directions

1. Choose a necklace and read the pattern beginning at the arrow.

2. Use the appropriate beads to complete the necklace by continuing the pattern.

3. Say the completed pattern.

4. Remove the beads and choose another necklace.

Nifty Necklaces *(cont.)*

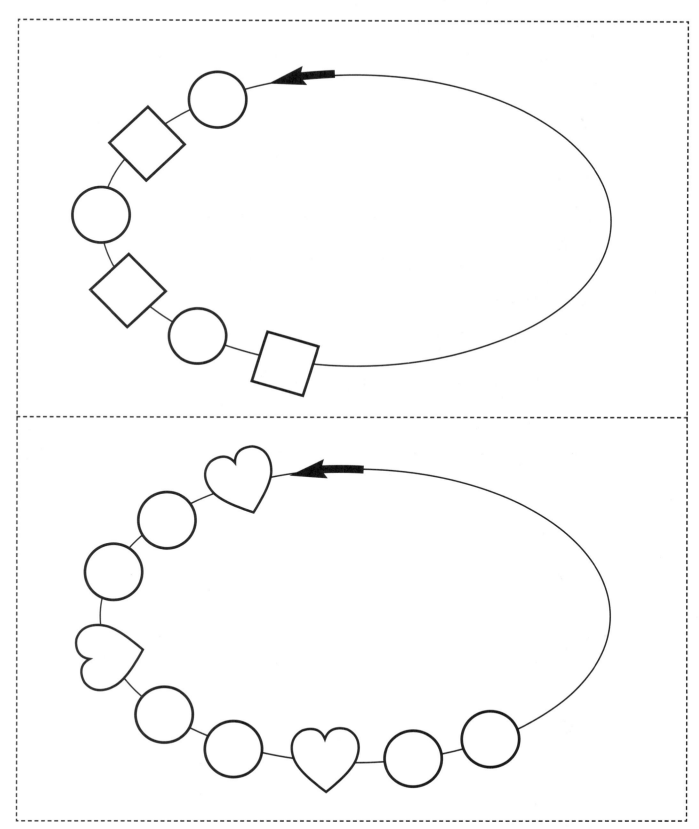

Nifty Necklaces *(cont.)*

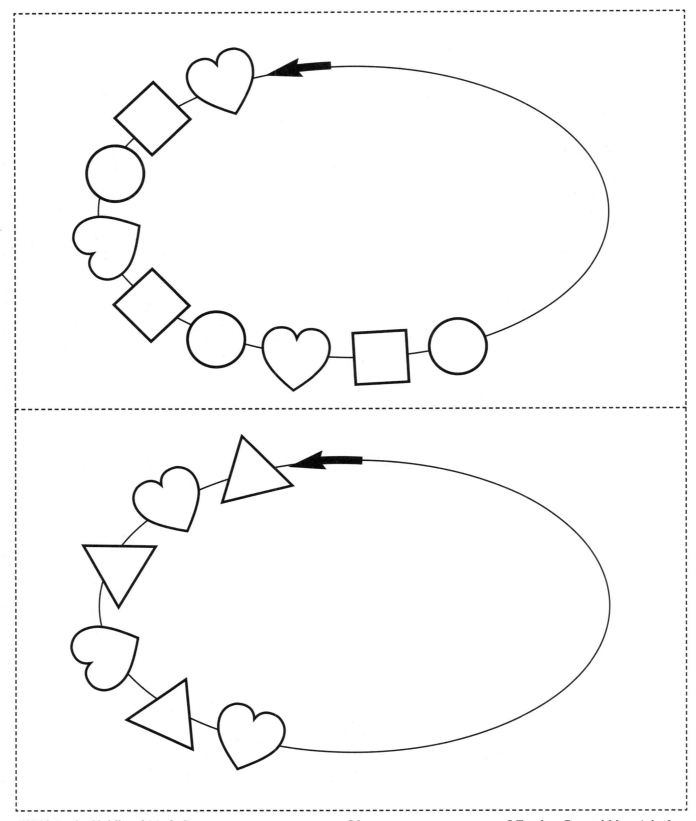

Nifty Necklaces *(cont.)*

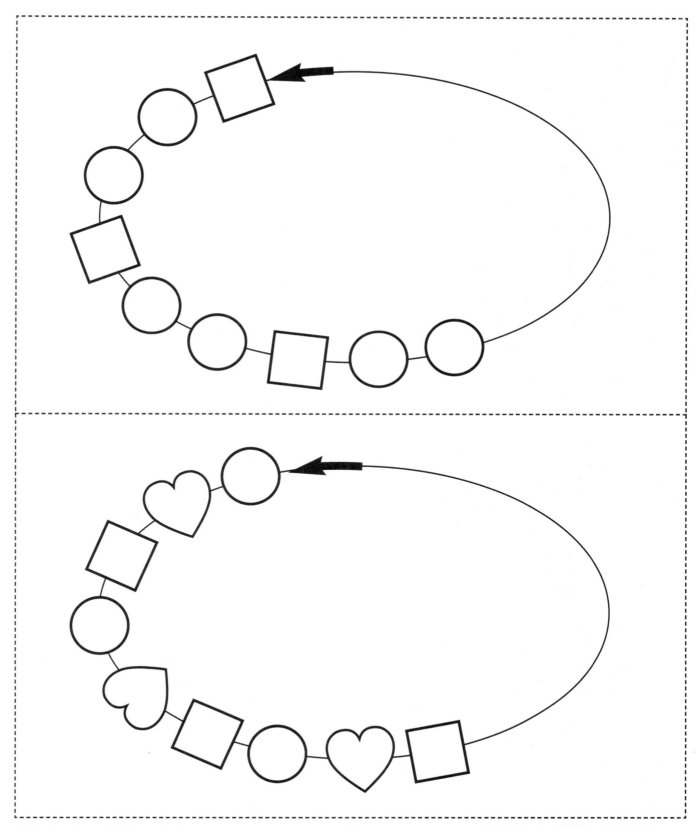

Nifty Necklaces *(cont.)*

Keep On Truckin'

Skill: Extending AB, ABB and ABC Patterns.

Materials: scissors; roads (pages 60–64); vehicles (page 65); tape

Teacher Preparation: Cut out roads and vehicles. Assemble two roads into one longer road by attaching the matching letters at the dots with tape. Color and laminate roads and vehicles, if desired.

Keep On Truckin'

Student Directions

1. Choose a road. Read the pattern starting at the arrow.

2. Say the completed pattern.

3. Repeat the pattern on the other side of the road.

4. Remove the vehicles and choose another road.

Keep On Truckin' *(cont.)*

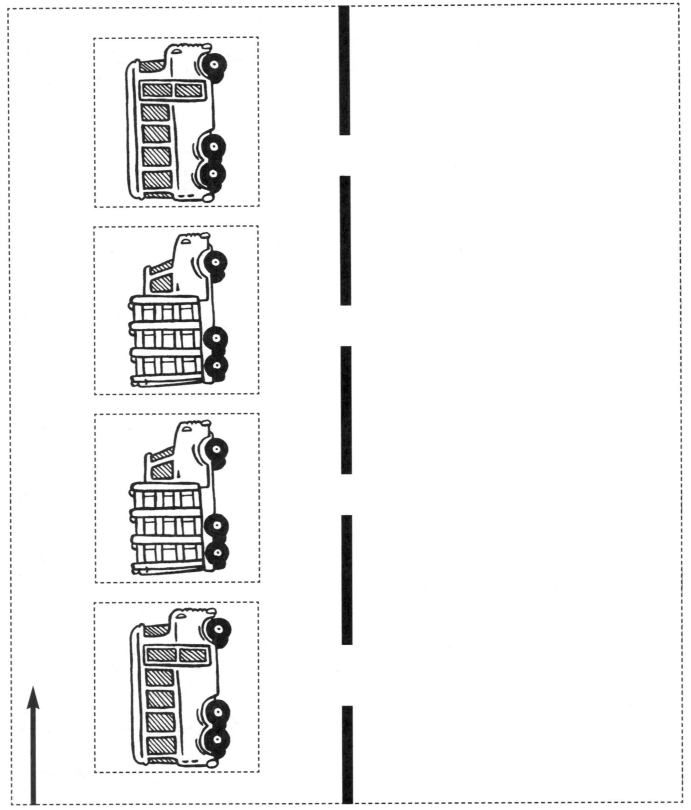

Keep On Truckin' *(cont.)*

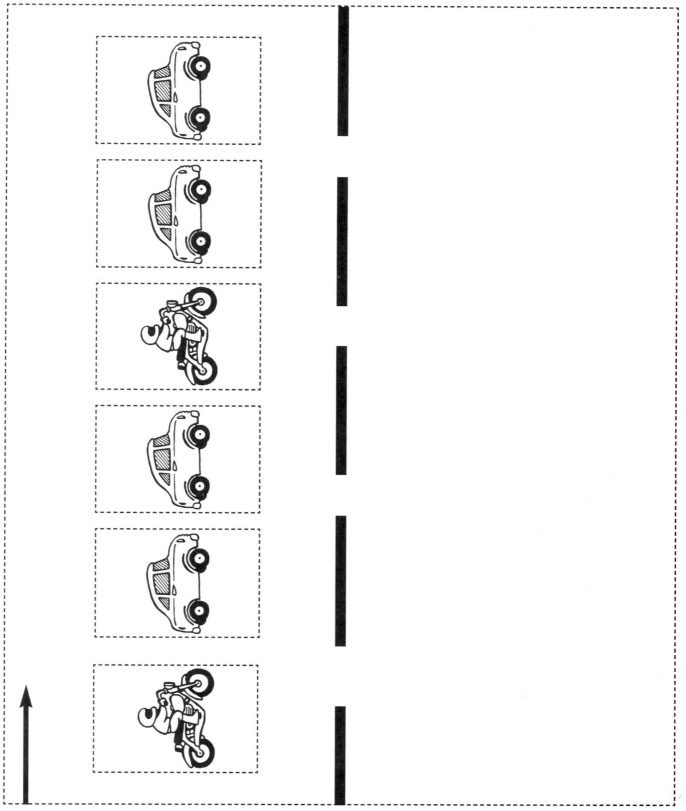

Keep On Truckin' *(cont.)*

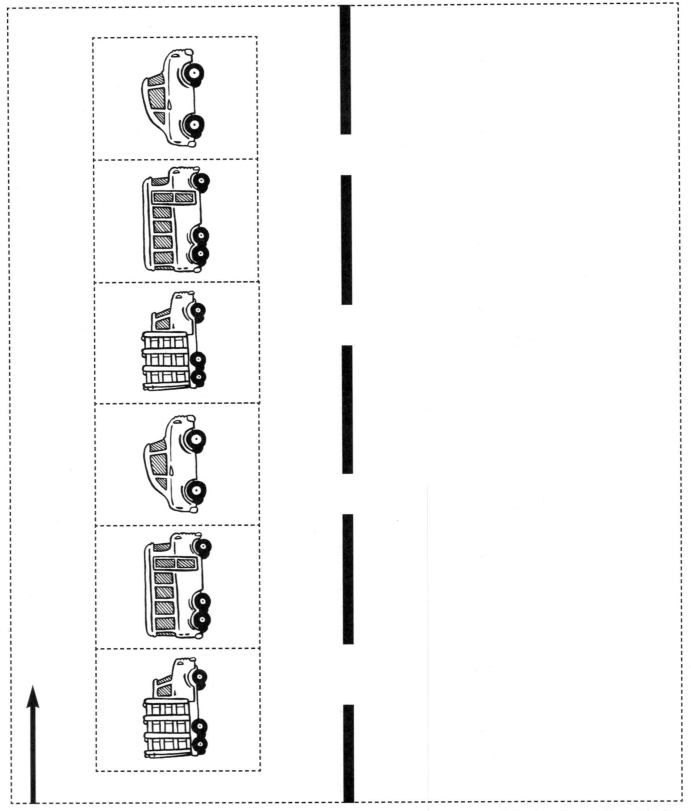

Keep On Truckin' *(cont.)*

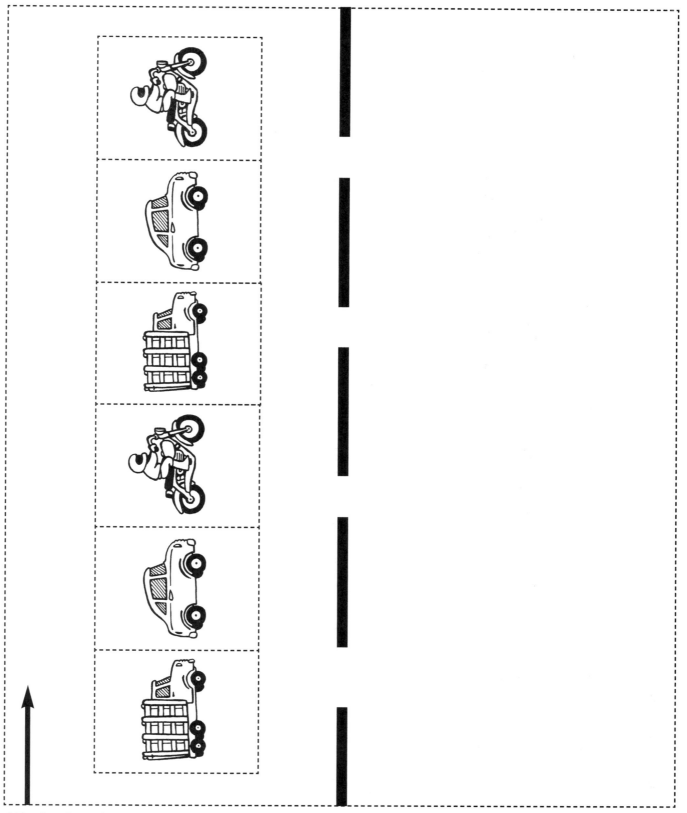

Keep On Truckin' *(cont.)*

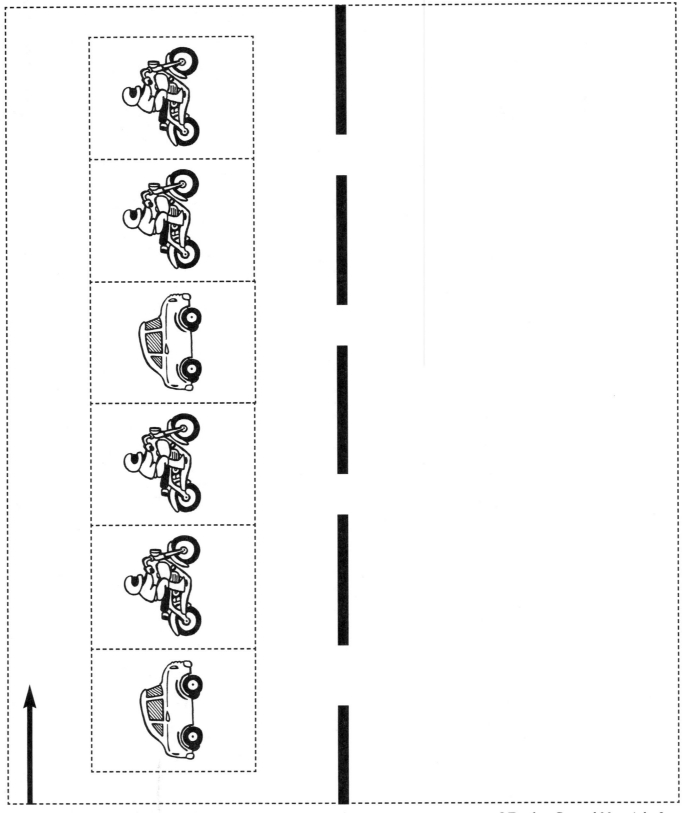

Keep On Truckin' *(cont.)*

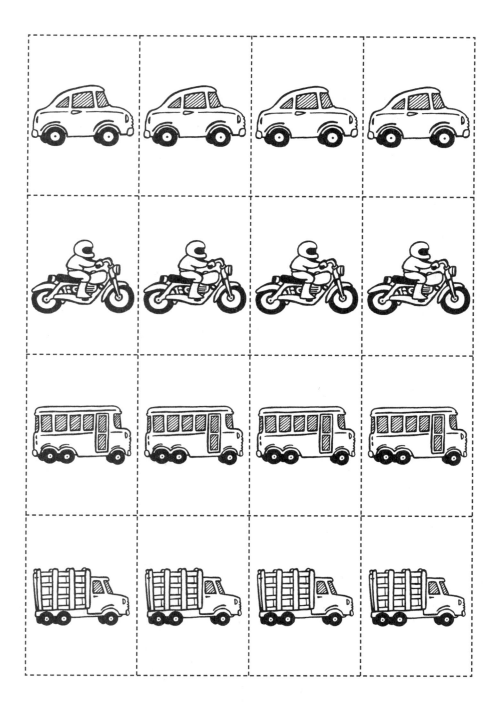

Flower Fun

Skill: Extending AB, ABB, AAB and ABC Patterns

Materials: scissors; flowers (page 70); gardens (pages 67–69)

Teacher Preparation: Color and laminate gardens and flowers, if desired. Cut out flowers.

Flower Fun

Student Directions

1. Choose a row of flowers. Look at the first pattern.

2. Extend the pattern using the appropriate flowers.

3. Continue until all patterns are complete.

4. Remove the flowers and choose another pattern to complete.

Flower Fun *(cont.)*

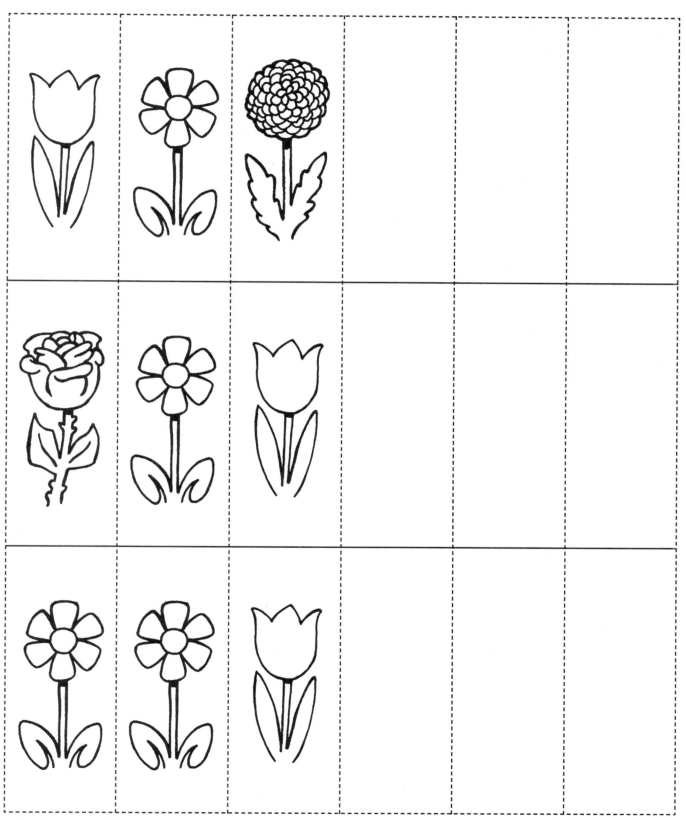

Flower Fun *(cont.)*

68

Flower Fun (cont.)

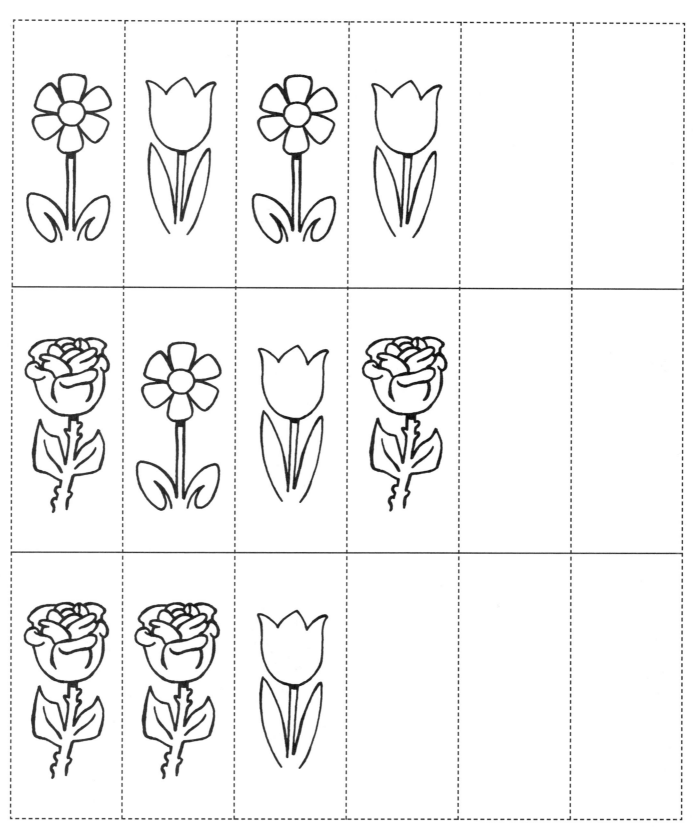

Flower Fun *(cont.)*

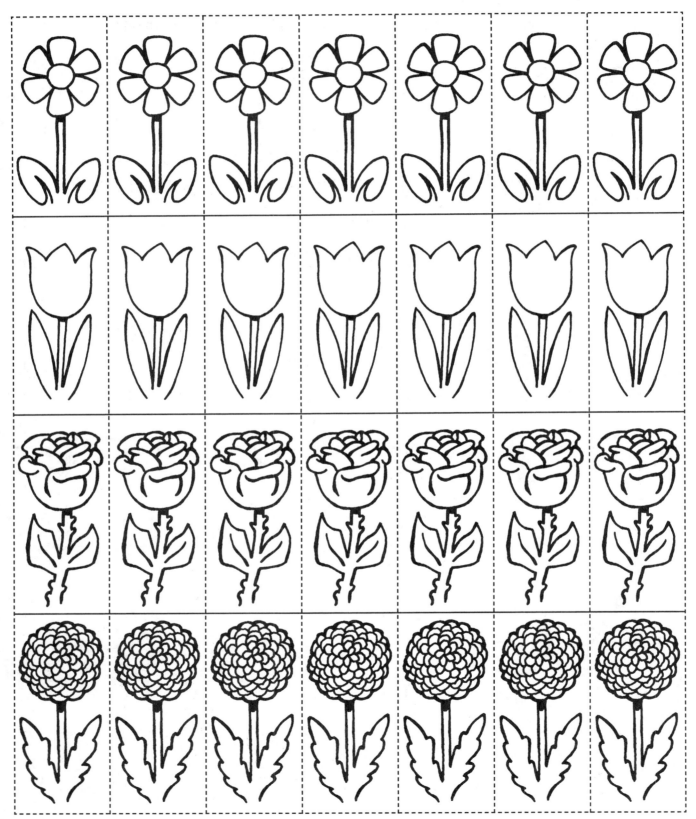

Pattern Sort

Skill: Identifying Patterns

Materials: scissors; pattern strips (pages 72–73); pattern mats (pages 74–75)

Teacher Preparation: Cut apart pattern strips. Laminate pattern strips and pattern mats, if desired.

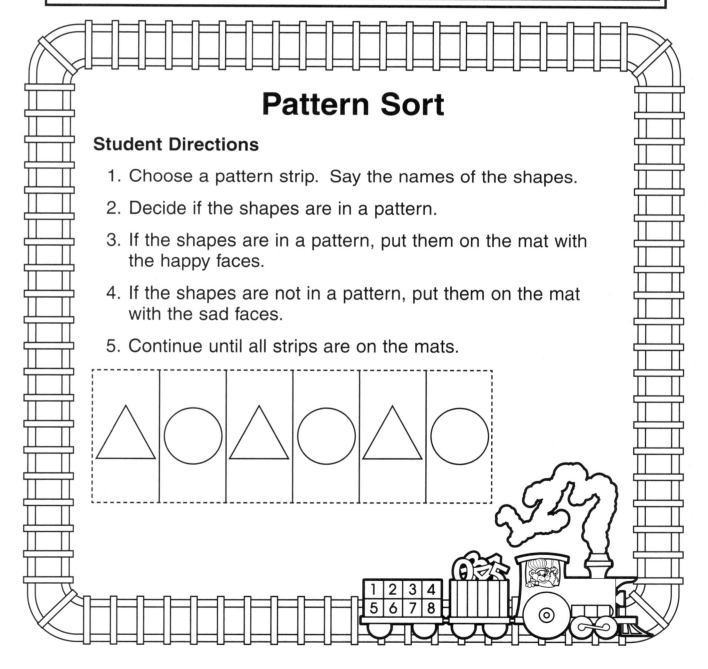

Pattern Sort

Student Directions

1. Choose a pattern strip. Say the names of the shapes.

2. Decide if the shapes are in a pattern.

3. If the shapes are in a pattern, put them on the mat with the happy faces.

4. If the shapes are not in a pattern, put them on the mat with the sad faces.

5. Continue until all strips are on the mats.

Pattern Sort (cont.)

Pattern Sort *(cont.)*

Pattern Sort *(cont.)*

Pattern Sort *(cont.)*

 #3718 Early Childhood Math Centers

Farm Animal Fun

Skill: Sorting, Classifying

Materials: scissors; animals (pages 77–78); animal homes (pages 79–82)

Teacher Preparation: Cut out animals on dotted lines. Color and laminate animals and animal homes, if desired.

Farm Animal Fun

Student Directions

1. Place the animal homes in front of you.

2. Choose an animal and put it in the correct home.

3. Continue until all animals have been placed in the correct home.

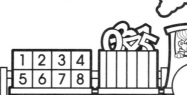

Farm Animal Fun *(cont.)*

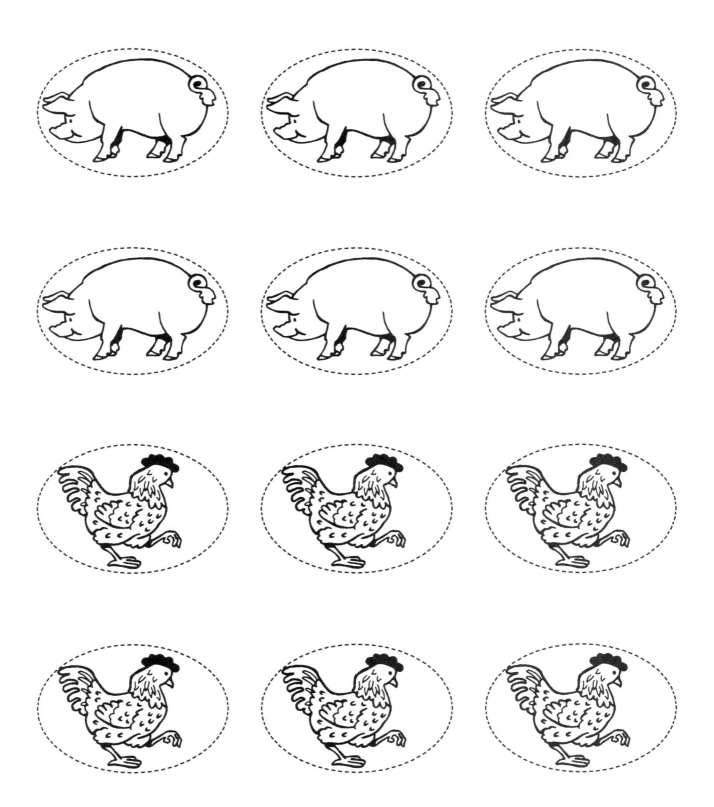

Farm Animal Fun *(cont.)*

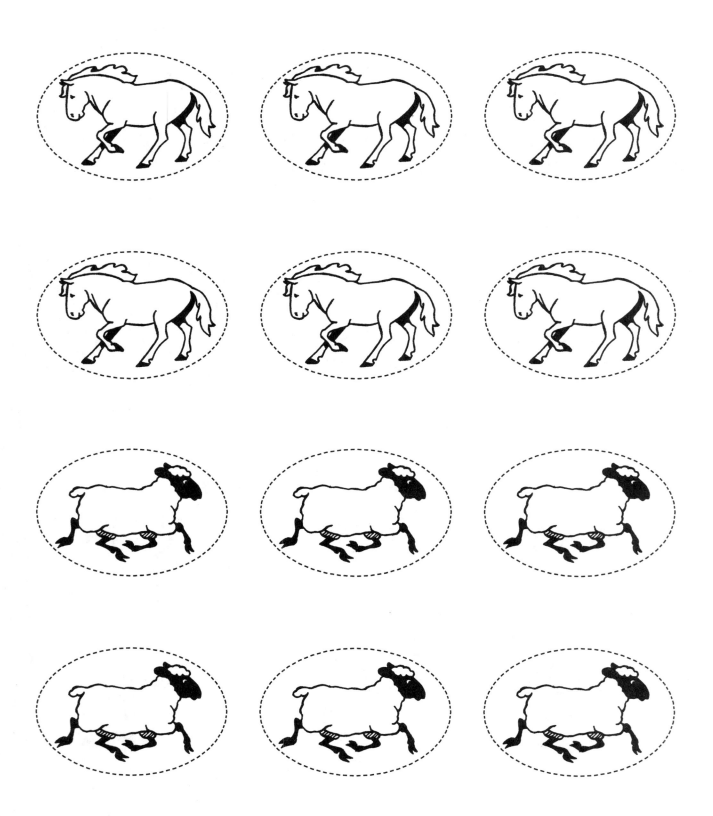

Farm Animal Fun *(cont.)*

Pig Pen

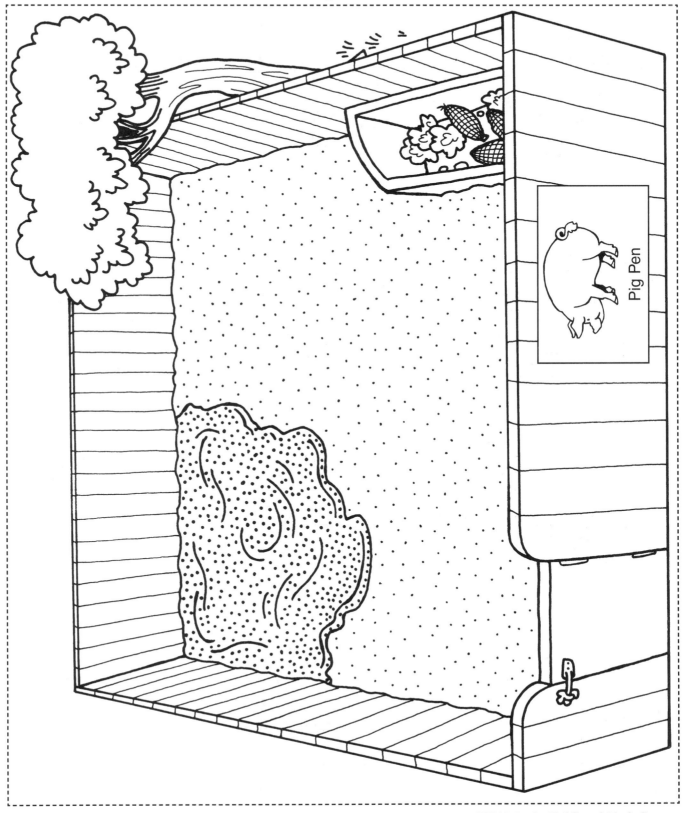

Farm Animal Fun *(cont.)*

Chicken Coop

Chicken Coop

Farm Animal Fun *(cont.)*

Horse Pasture

Farm Animal Fun *(cont.)*

Sheep Pen

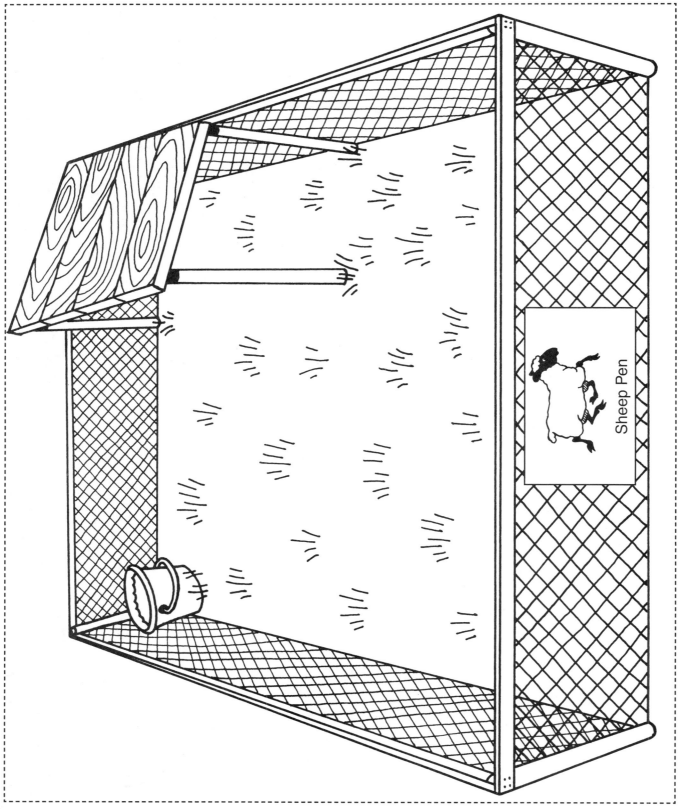

Backwards Bingo

Skill: Sorting Colors

Materials: bingo card (page 84); color cards (page 85); scissors

Teacher Preparation: Reproduce a sufficient number of bingo cards and color cards for the number of children in the center. Color the color cards and the top of each column of the bingo card the color indicated on the label. Cut out the color cards. Laminate the bingo cards and color cards, if desired.

Backwards Bingo

Student Directions

1. Choose a bingo card. Place it in front of you.

2. Mix up the color cards and place them face down in front of you.

3. Choose a color card and put it in any square of the correct color column on the bingo card.

4. Continue until you have four in a row in any direction.

5. If you are playing with other children, each player takes a turn choosing a color card until someone gets a bingo.

6. Remove the color cards and start again.

Backwards Bingo *(cont.)*

				Red
				Yellow
				Green
				Blue

84

Backwards Bingo *(cont.)*

Red	Red	Red	Red
Yellow	Yellow	Yellow	Yellow
Green	Green	Green	Green
Blue	Blue	Blue	Blue

Book Bonanza

Skill: Sorting and Classifying Books

Materials: scissors; book bins (pages 87–90); book reproducible (pages 91–92); pencil

Teacher Preparation: Cut out books. Color and laminate books and book bins, if desired. Write the name of the correct book bin on the back of each book for student self-checking.

Book Bonanza

Student Directions

1. Place the four book bins in front of you. Put the books in a pile.

2. Choose a book and decide which bin it belongs in. Use the pictures on the book and the book bin label to help you choose the correct bin.

3. Put the book in the correct bin and choose another book.

4. Continue until all books have been put into the correct book bin.

5. Check your work by looking at the word written on the back of each book to see if it matches the one on the bin you have chosen.

Book Bonanza *(cont.)*

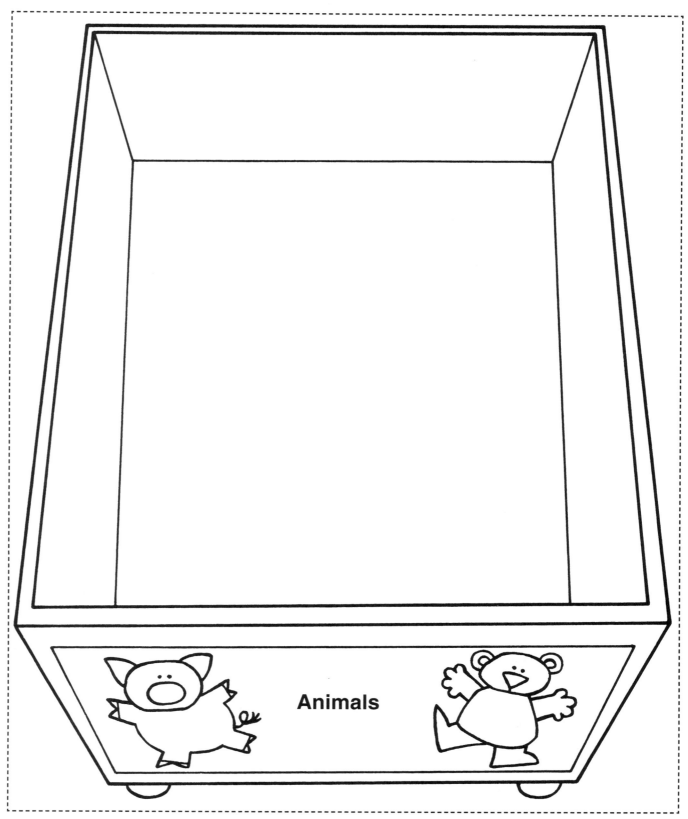

Animals

Book Bonanza *(cont.)*

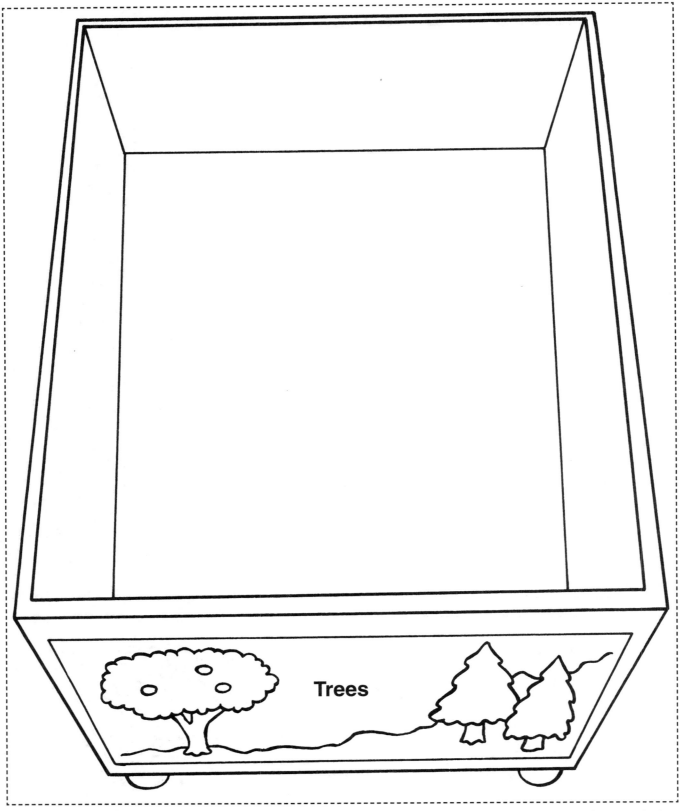

Trees

88

Book Bonanza *(cont.)*

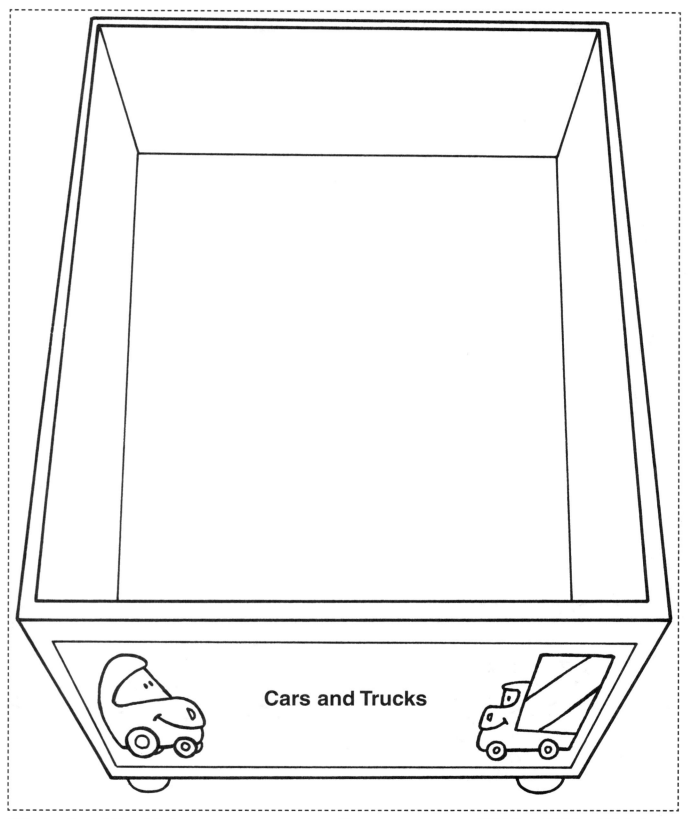

Cars and Trucks

Book Bonanza *(cont.)*

Insects

Book Bonanza *(cont.)*

Book Bonanza *(cont.)*

Zany Zebras

Skill: Sorting, Classifying

Materials: scissors; zebras (pages 94–97); sorting mats (pages 98–101)

Teacher Preparation: Cut out zebras. Laminate zebras and sorting mats, if desired.

Zany Zebras

Student Directions

1. Lay the sorting mats in front of you. Put the zebras in a pile.

2. Choose a zebra and look at the design on its back.

3. Find the sorting mat that has the same design and put the zebra on that mat.

4. Choose another zebra and continue until all zebras have been put on the correct sorting mat.

Zany Zebras *(cont.)*

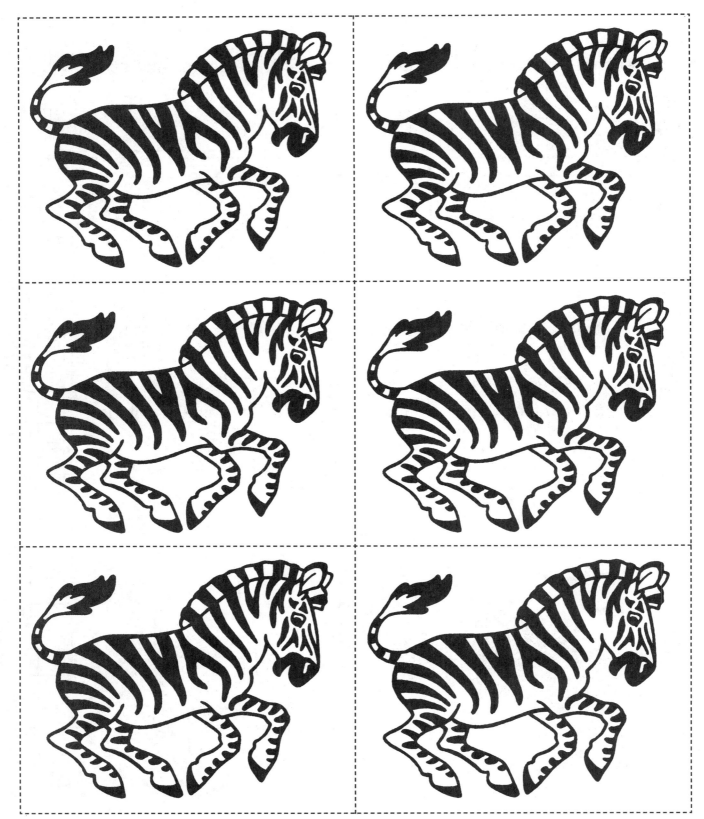

94

Zany Zebras *(cont.)*

Zany Zebras (cont.)

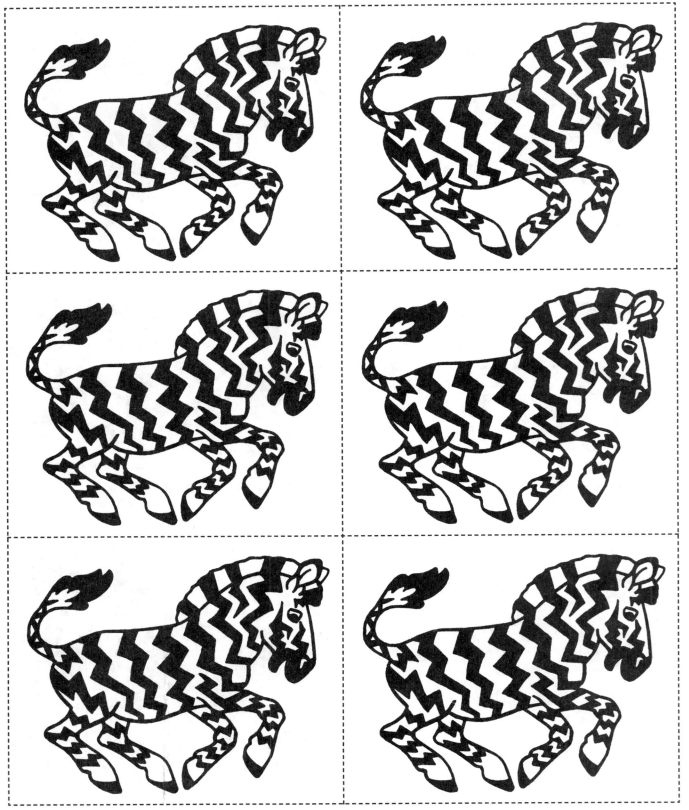

Zany Zebras (cont.)

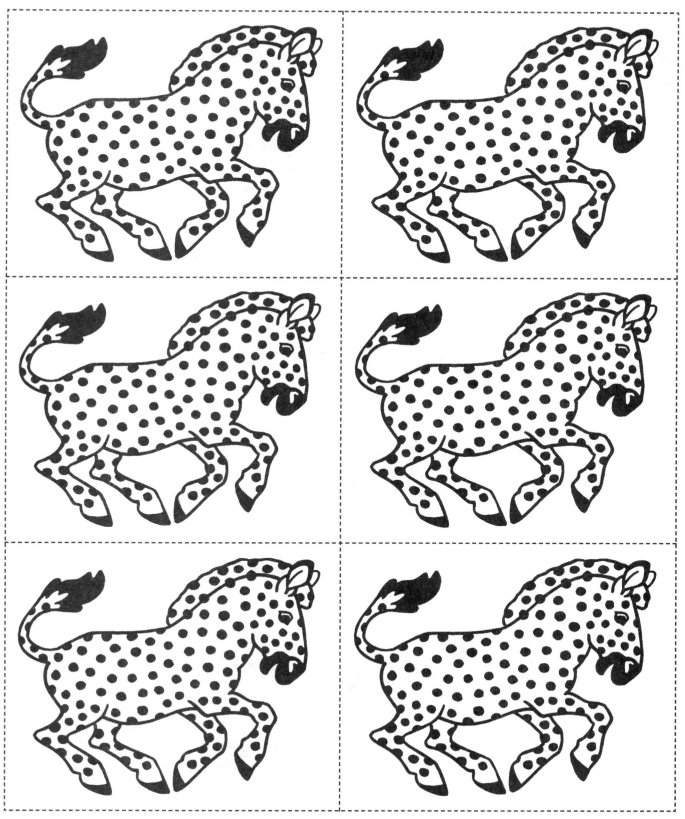

Zany Zebras *(cont.)*

Zany Zebras *(cont.)*

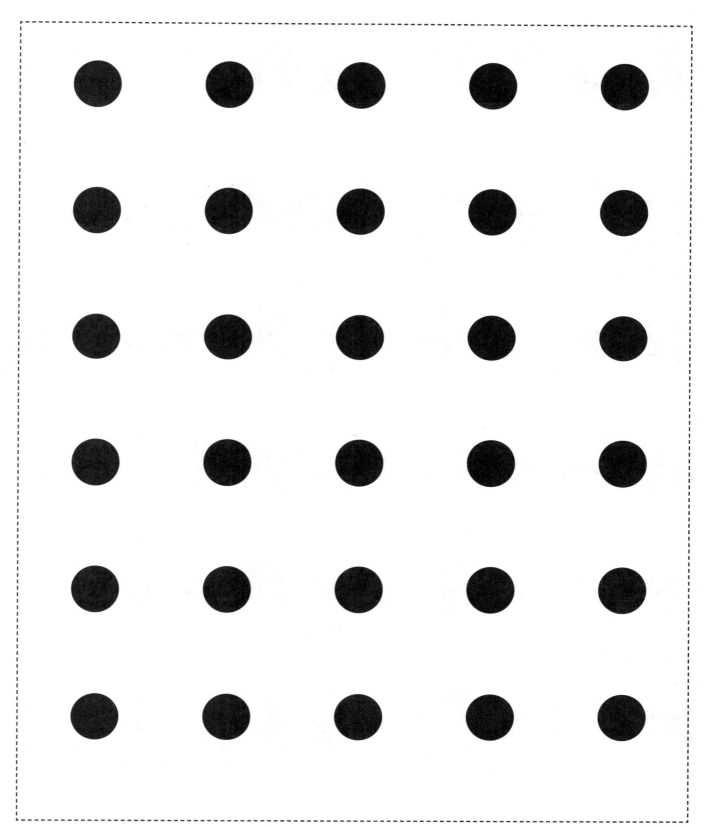

Zany Zebras *(cont.)*

Zany Zebras *(cont.)*

Shoe Sort

Skill: Sorting, Classifying

Materials: scissors; shoe racks (pages 103–105); shoes (page 106), two copies

Teacher Preparation: Cut out shoes. Color and laminate shoe racks and shoes, if desired.

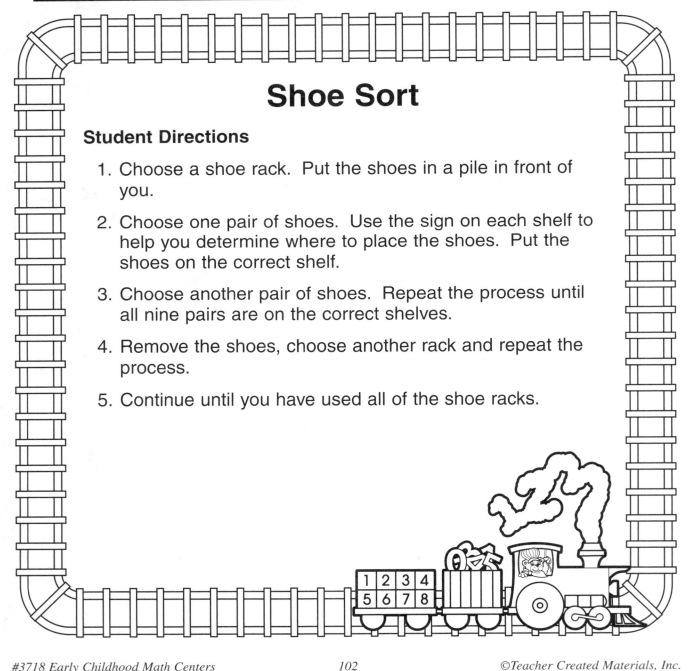

Shoe Sort

Student Directions

1. Choose a shoe rack. Put the shoes in a pile in front of you.

2. Choose one pair of shoes. Use the sign on each shelf to help you determine where to place the shoes. Put the shoes on the correct shelf.

3. Choose another pair of shoes. Repeat the process until all nine pairs are on the correct shelves.

4. Remove the shoes, choose another rack and repeat the process.

5. Continue until you have used all of the shoe racks.

Shoe Sort *(cont.)*

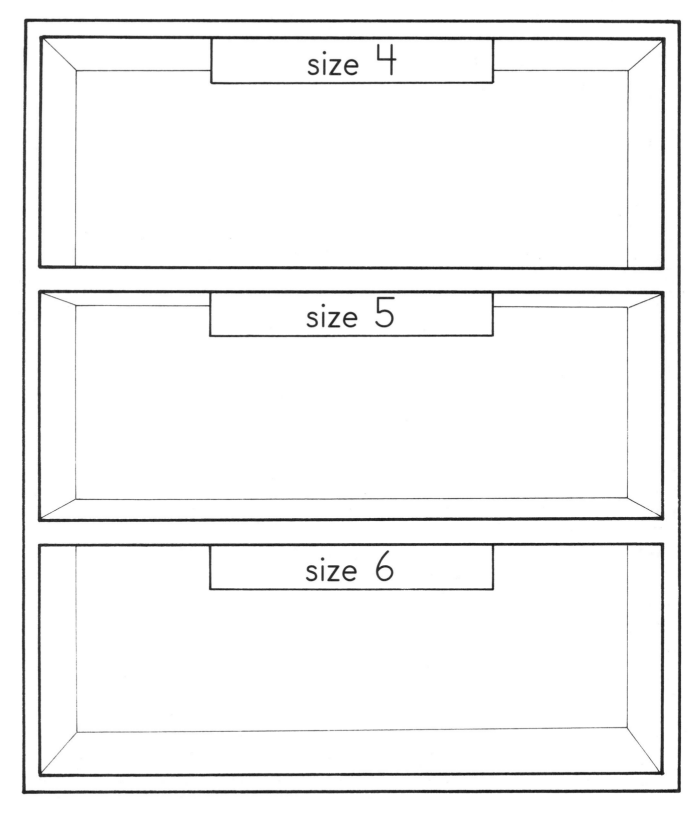

Shoe Sort *(cont.)*

Shoe Sort *(cont.)*

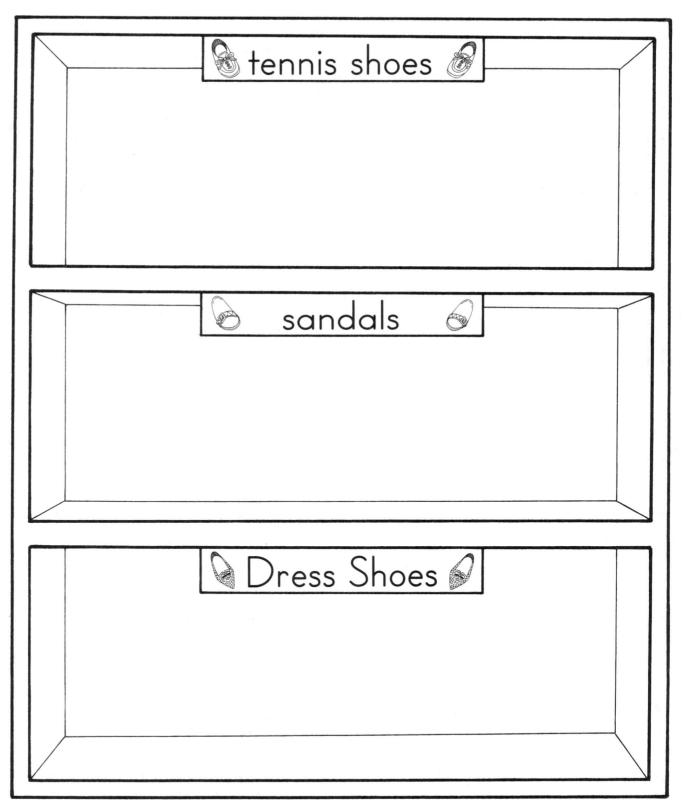

tennis shoes

sandals

Dress Shoes

Shoe Sort *(cont.)*

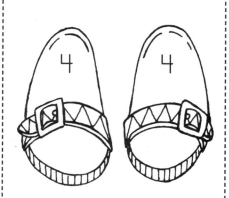 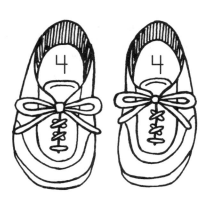  

 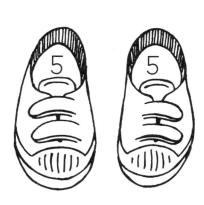 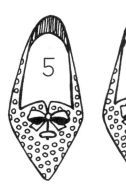 

 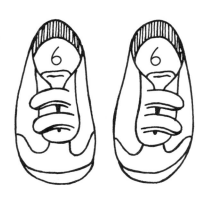  

Class Sort

Skill: Sorting and Classifying

Materials: student cards (page 108); sorting mats (pages 109–111); letter strips (pages 112–114); scissors; tape

Teacher Preparation: Reproduce enough student cards to have one for each student in your class. Have each student in your class complete student card with his or her hair and eye color. Have each student write his or her name on the line at the bottom of the card. If you will have more than one student in the center at a time, you will need a set of student cards for each child working at the center. (For example, if you have three children working in the center at a time, you will need each child to complete three student cards to make three complete class sets.) Cut out the letter strips and assemble them into one long alphabet by connecting them with tape. Put the student cards along with the sorting mats and letter strip in the center. Color the eyes and hair on the sorting mats the indicated color.

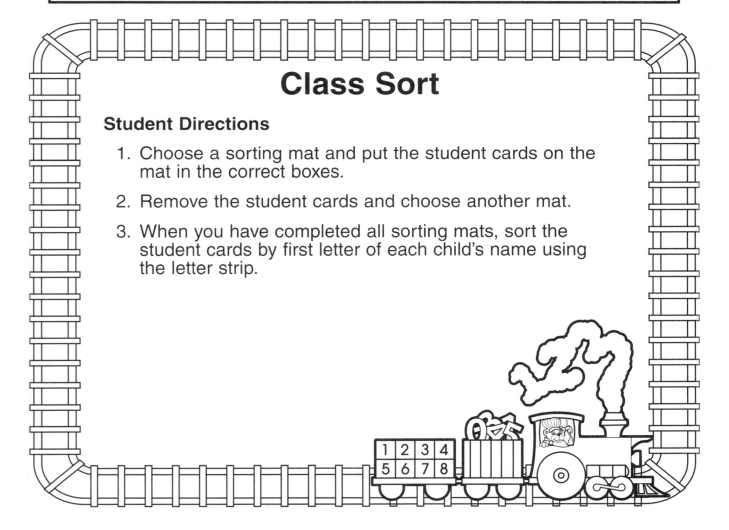

Class Sort

Student Directions

1. Choose a sorting mat and put the student cards on the mat in the correct boxes.

2. Remove the student cards and choose another mat.

3. When you have completed all sorting mats, sort the student cards by first letter of each child's name using the letter strip.

Class Sort *(cont.)*

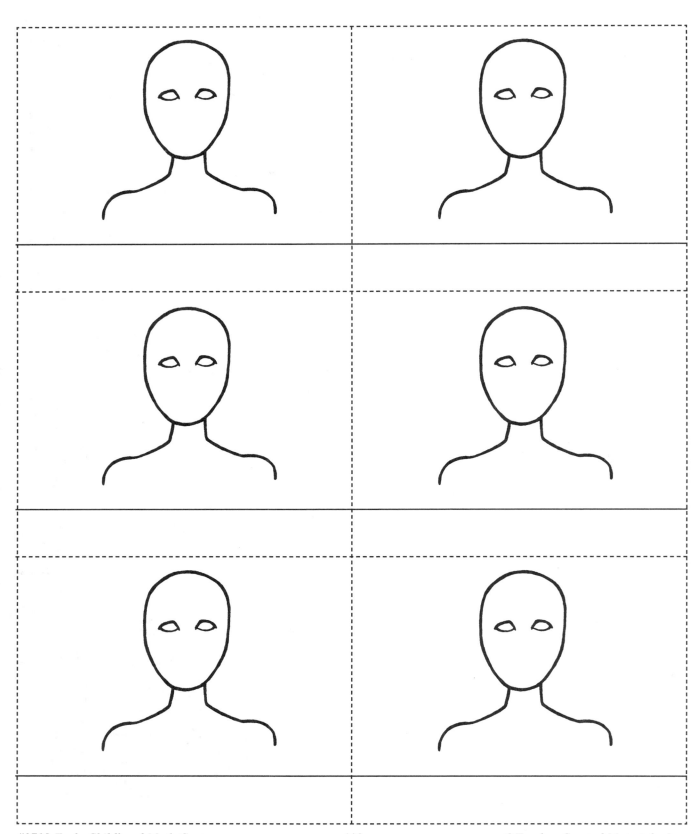

Class Sort *(cont.)*

👁 blue eyes 👁	👁 brown eyes 👁
👁 green eyes 👁	👁 black eyes 👁

Class Sort *(cont.)*

brown hair	black hair

blond hair	red hair

Class Sort *(cont.)*

 boys

 girls

Class Sort *(cont.)*

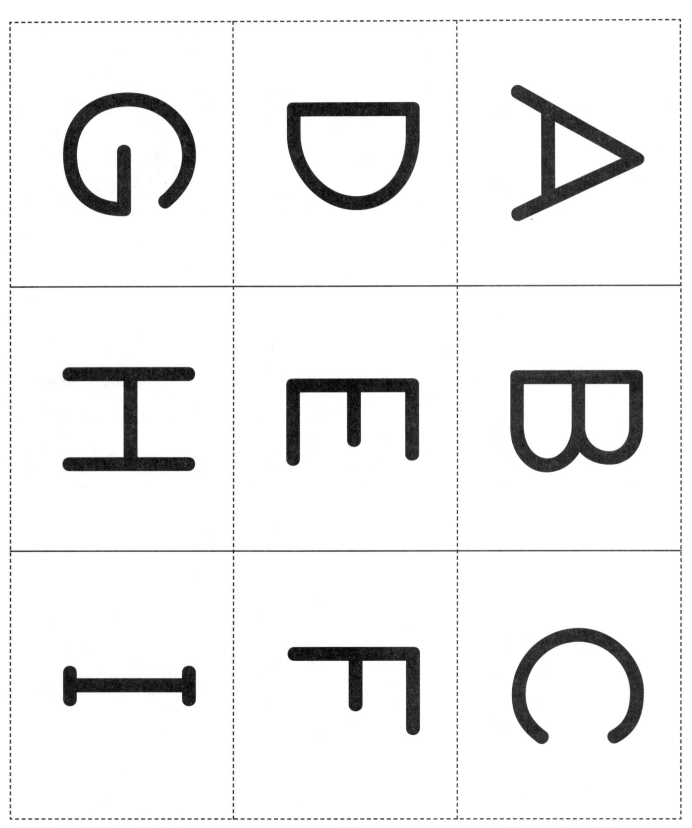

Class Sort *(cont.)*

P	M	U
Q	N	K
R	O	L

Class Sort *(cont.)*

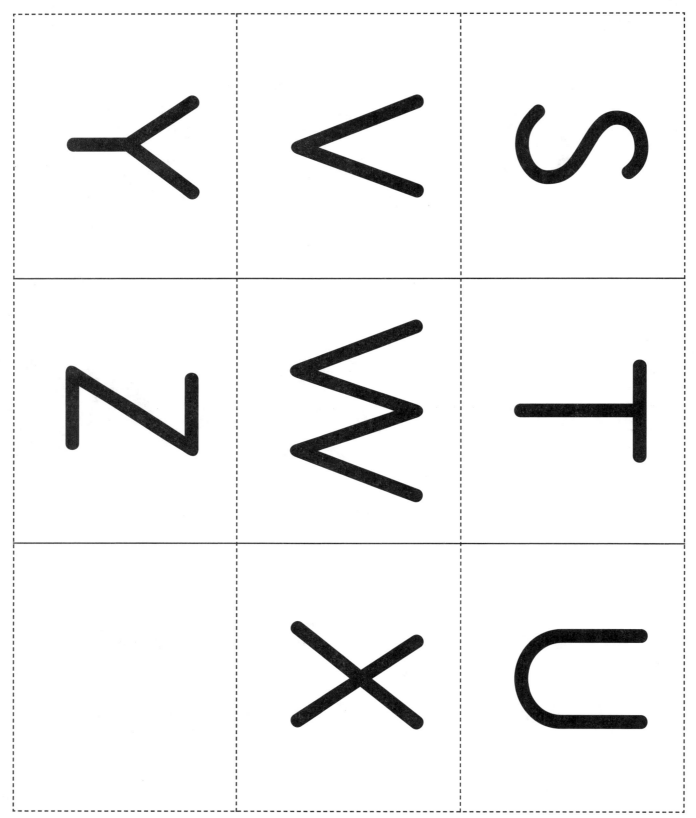

Shape Puzzles

Skill: Recognizing and Assembling Shapes

Materials: scissors; shape puzzles (pages 116–120); envelopes; pencil

Teacher Preparation: Cut out each shape puzzle. Color and laminate the puzzles, if desired. Put the pieces of each puzzle in a separate envelope and label the outside of each with the appropriate shape. Label the back of each puzzle piece with the correct shape to help keep puzzle pieces organized.

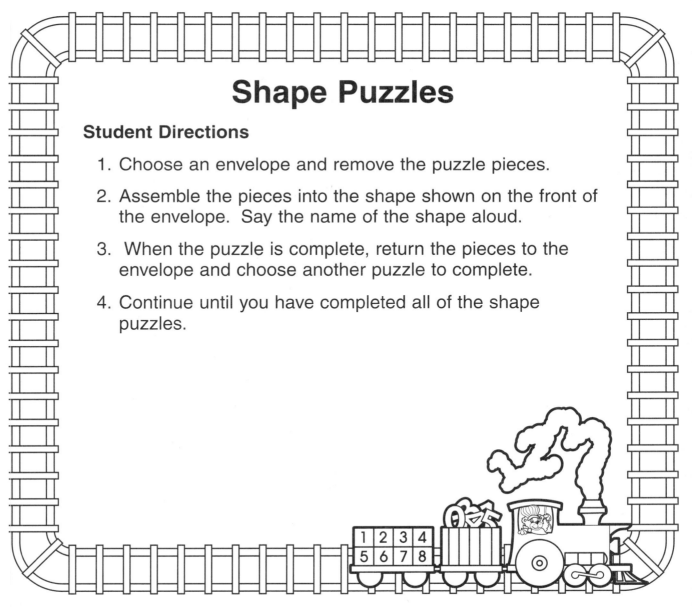

Shape Puzzles

Student Directions

1. Choose an envelope and remove the puzzle pieces.

2. Assemble the pieces into the shape shown on the front of the envelope. Say the name of the shape aloud.

3. When the puzzle is complete, return the pieces to the envelope and choose another puzzle to complete.

4. Continue until you have completed all of the shape puzzles.

Shape Puzzles *(cont.)*

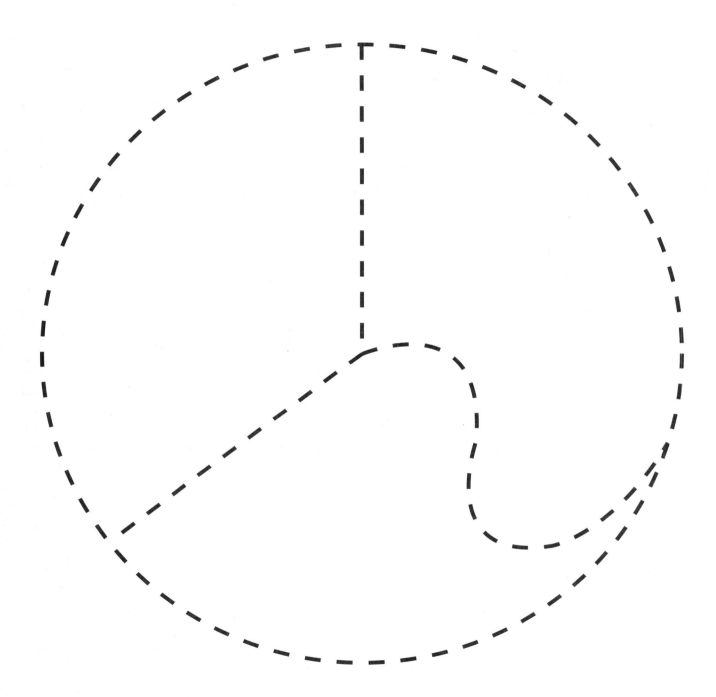

Shape Puzzles *(cont.)*

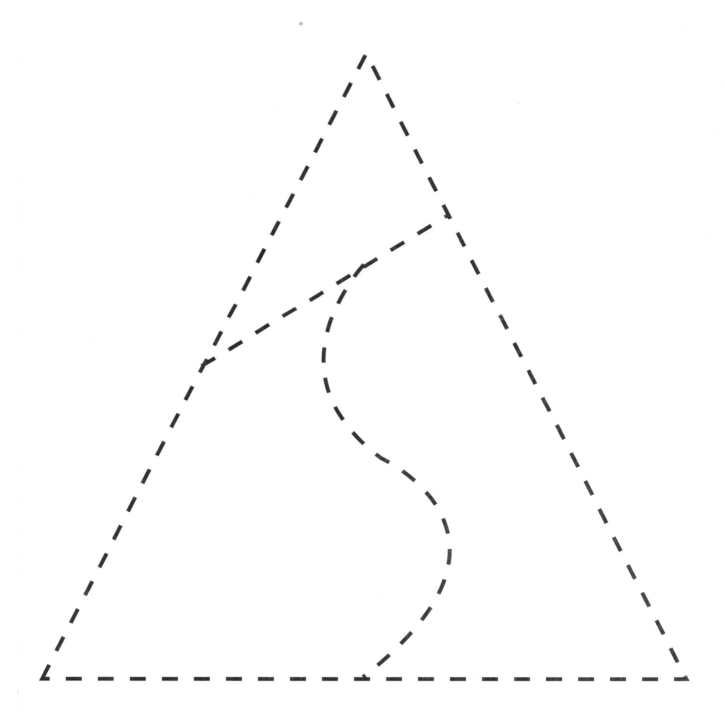

Shape Puzzles *(cont.)*

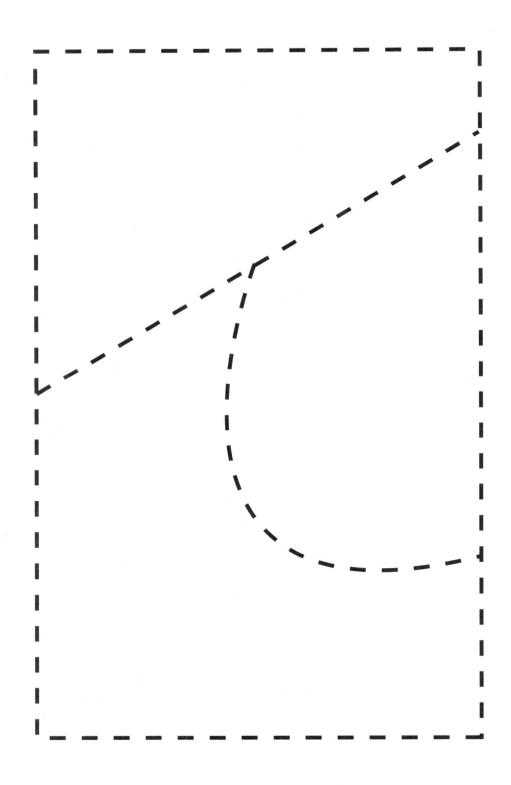

Shape Puzzles *(cont.)*

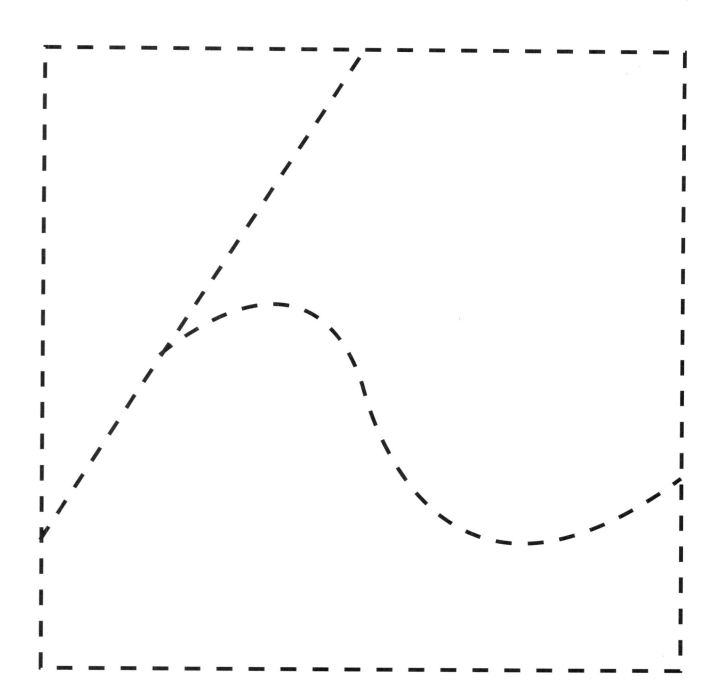

Shape Puzzles *(cont.)*

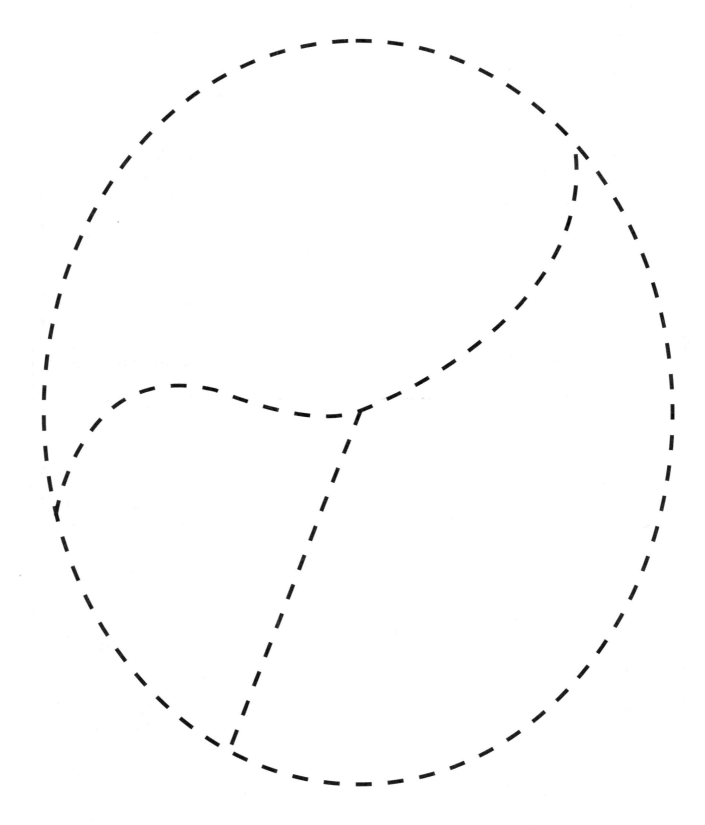

Start Your Engines

Skill: Matching Shapes

Materials: scissors; cars (pages 122–123); keys (page 124)

Teacher Preparation: Cut out the cars and the keys. Color and laminate cars and keys, if desired.

Start Your Engines

Student Directions

1. Place the cars and keys in front of you.

2. Choose a car. Find the key that has the same shape on it.

3. Put the key on the car.

4. Choose another car and continue until all the cars are matched with the correct key.

Start Your Engines *(cont.)*

Start Your Engines *(cont.)*

Start Your Engines *(cont.)*

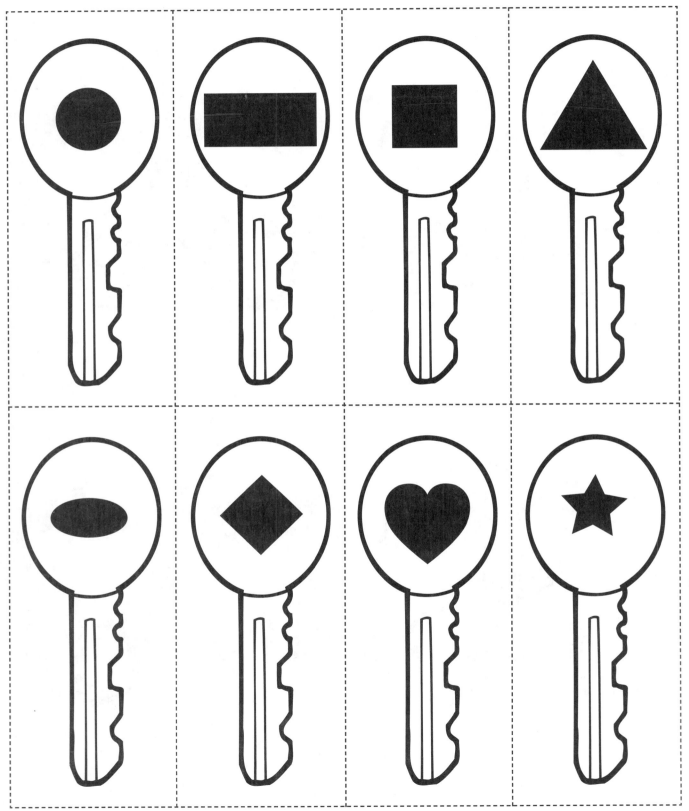

In Shape!

Skill: Shape and Size Matching

Materials: game cards (pages 126–129); shape cutouts (page 130); scissors; envelopes

Teacher Preparation: Make one copy of the shape cutouts for each child at the center. Cut out the shapes and put the set in an envelope. Label the back of each piece in a set with a letter or color dot to help keep them organized. Color and laminate the game cards and shape cutouts, if desired.

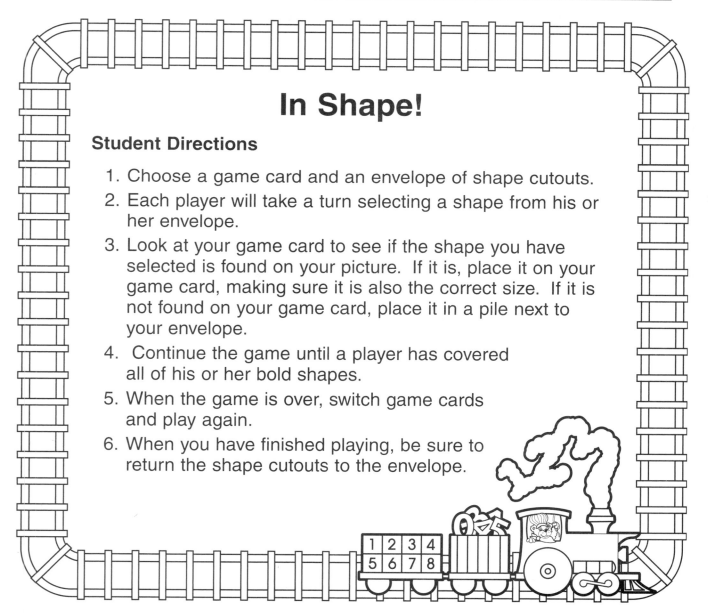

In Shape!

Student Directions

1. Choose a game card and an envelope of shape cutouts.
2. Each player will take a turn selecting a shape from his or her envelope.
3. Look at your game card to see if the shape you have selected is found on your picture. If it is, place it on your game card, making sure it is also the correct size. If it is not found on your game card, place it in a pile next to your envelope.
4. Continue the game until a player has covered all of his or her bold shapes.
5. When the game is over, switch game cards and play again.
6. When you have finished playing, be sure to return the shape cutouts to the envelope.

In Shape! *(cont.)*

126

In Shape! *(cont.)*

In Shape! *(cont.)*

In Shape! *(cont.)*

In Shape! *(cont.)*

130

Shapes Everywhere

Skill: Matching Shapes, Fine Motor Development

Materials: scissors; mini-book pages (pages 132–135); shape pictures (page 136); glue

Teacher Preparation: Assemble a mini book for each student. Copy the mini book pages, cut the pages on the dotted lines and staple them together in the correct order. Copy the shape pictures page for each student.

Shapes Everywhere

Student Directions

1. Cut out the shape pictures on the dotted lines on the shape pictures page.

2. Write your name in the space provided on the cover of the mini book.

3. Turn to page one and look at the shape at the top of the page.

4. Find the shape picture that is the same as the shape at the top of the page. Glue it in the dotted box at the bottom of the page.

5. Continue until all of the pages in the mini book are completed.

6. Read your book if there is time.

Shapes Everywhere *(cont.)*

Shapes
Everywhere

By: _____

circle — ◯

A doughnut  and a [ ] are **circles**.

①

Shapes Everywhere *(cont.)*

square —

A calendar

January						
S	M	T	W	Th	F	S
	1	2	3	4	5	6
7	8	9	10	11	12	13
14	15	16	17	18	19	20
21	22	23	24	25	26	27
28	29	30	31			

and a are **squares.**

②

triangle —

A slice of pizza  and a are **triangles.**

③

Shapes Everywhere *(cont.)*

rectangle —

A book  and a [ ] are **rectangles.**

④

oval —

A watermelon and an [ ] are **ovals.**

⑤

Shapes Everywhere *(cont.)*

heart —

A valentine  and a [ ] are **hearts**.

⑥

diamond —

A street sign  and a [ ] are **diamonds**.

⑦

Shapes Everywhere *(cont.)*

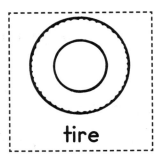
tire

window

wedge of
cheese

door

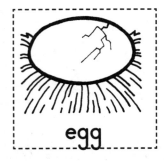
egg

necklace

kite

136

Cookie Time

Skill: Shape Matching

Materials: scissors; serving trays (pages 138–140); cookies (pages 141–143)

Teacher Preparation: Cut out the cookies. Color and laminate serving trays and cookies, if desired.

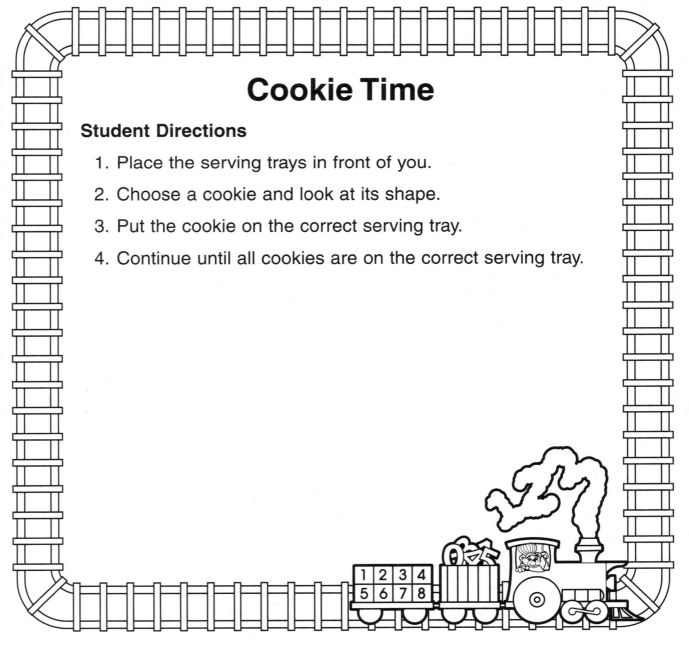

Cookie Time

Student Directions

1. Place the serving trays in front of you.

2. Choose a cookie and look at its shape.

3. Put the cookie on the correct serving tray.

4. Continue until all cookies are on the correct serving tray.

Cookie Time *(cont.)*

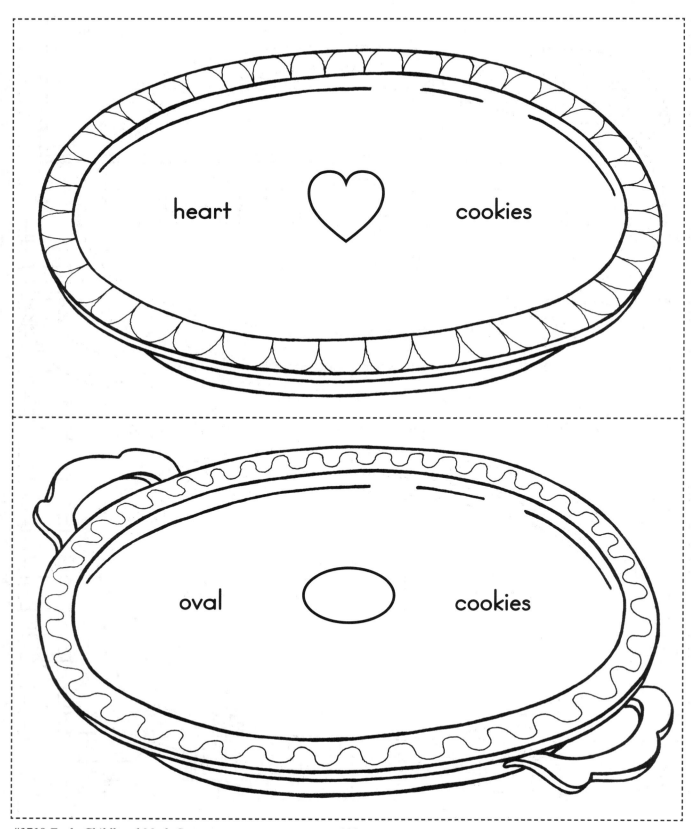

heart ♥ cookies

oval ⬭ cookies

Cookie Time *(cont.)*

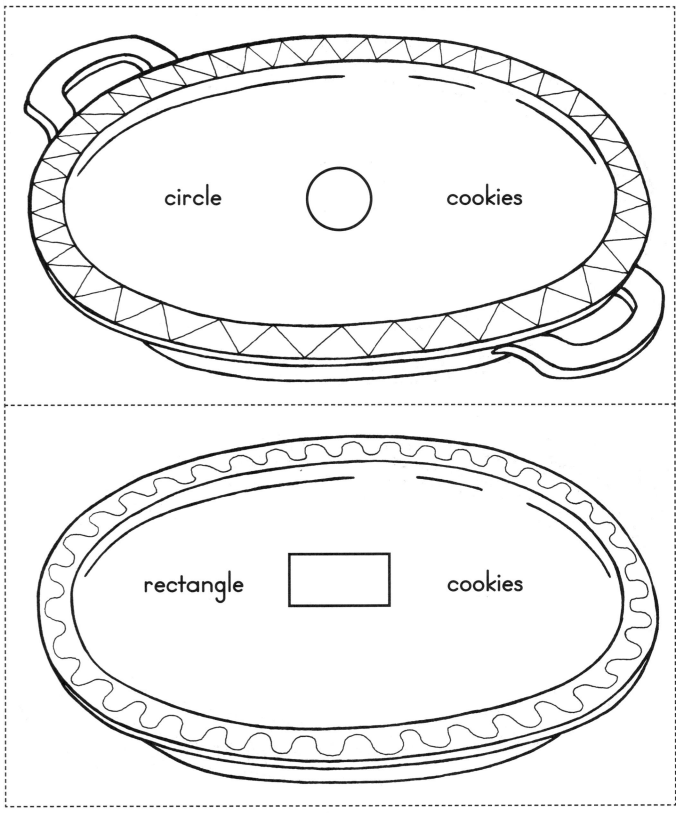

circle   cookies

rectangle   cookies

Cookie Time *(cont.)*

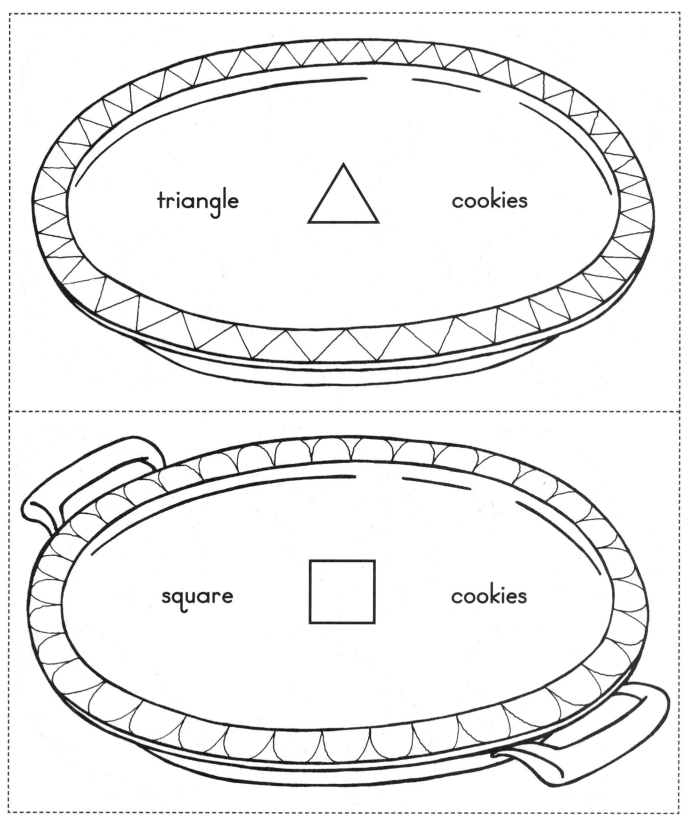

triangle   cookies

square   cookies

Cookie Time *(cont.)*

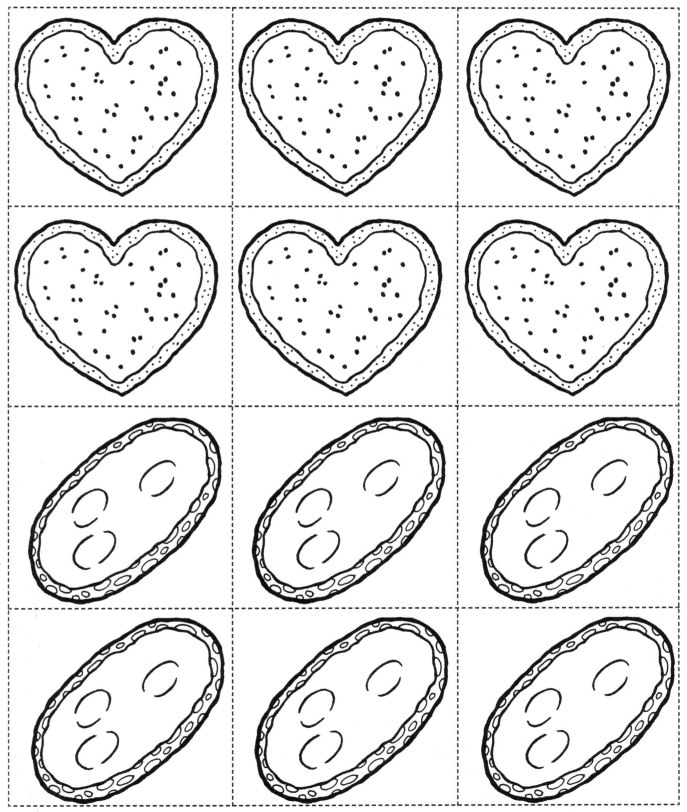

Cookie Time *(cont.)*

Cookie Time *(cont.)*

Trace the Tracks

Skill: Drawing Shapes, Fine Motor

Materials: scissors; tracks (pages 145–149); trains (page 150); tape

Teacher Preparation: Cut out tracks and trains. Color and laminate if desired. Students will need assistance or a demonstration on how to tape the trains to their fingers. (See illustration below.)

Trace the Tracks

Student Directions

1. Have a teacher or friend help you tape a train to your pointer finger so the wheels are just above your fingertip.

2. Choose a track and move your train around the track by tracing the shape with your finger.

3. As you trace the track, say the name of the shape you are tracing with your finger and your train.

4. After you are comfortable making that shape, choose another track and repeat the process.

5. Continue until you have traced all of the tracks.

Trace the Track *(cont.)*

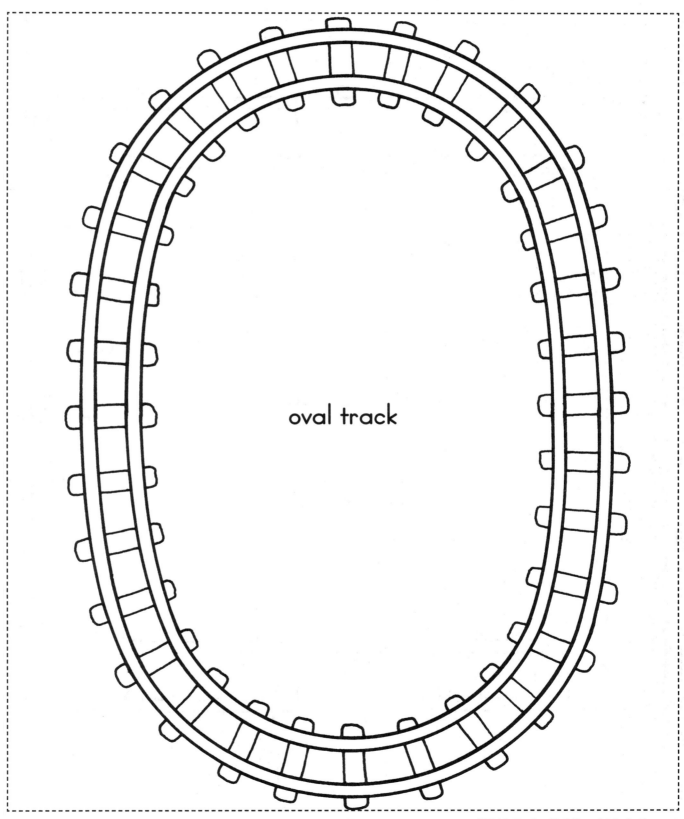

oval track

Trace the Track *(cont.)*

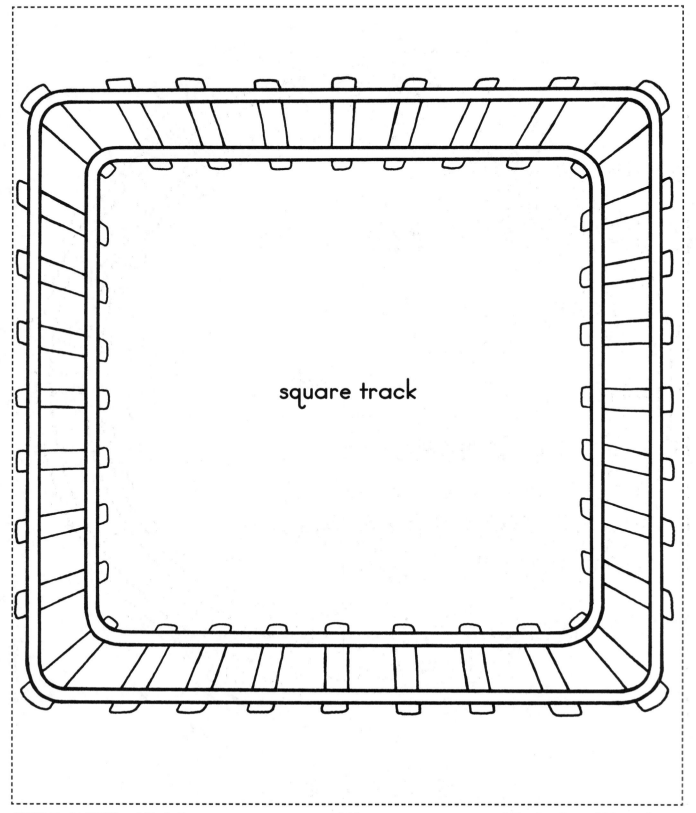

square track

Trace the Track *(cont.)*

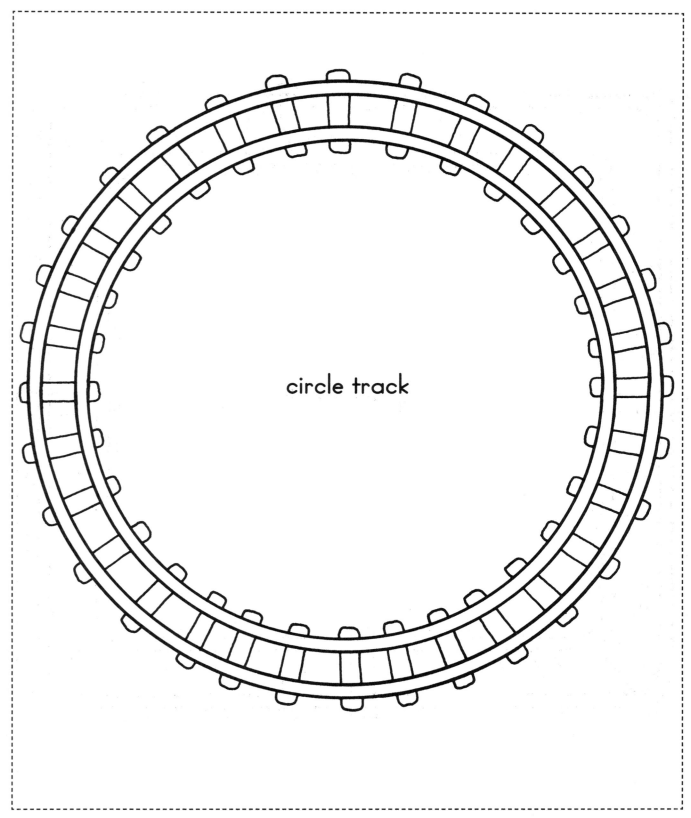

circle track

Trace the Track *(cont.)*

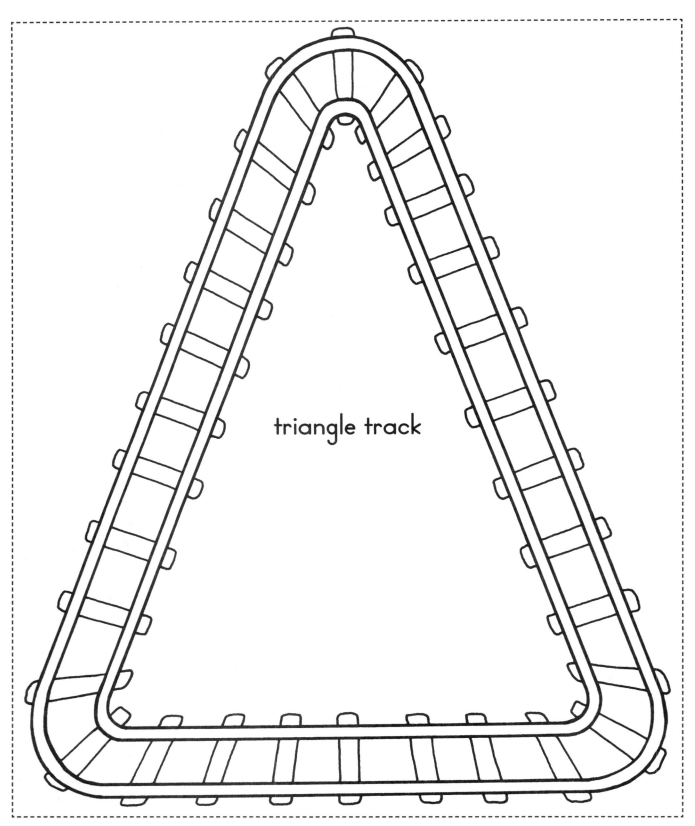

triangle track

Trace the Track *(cont.)*

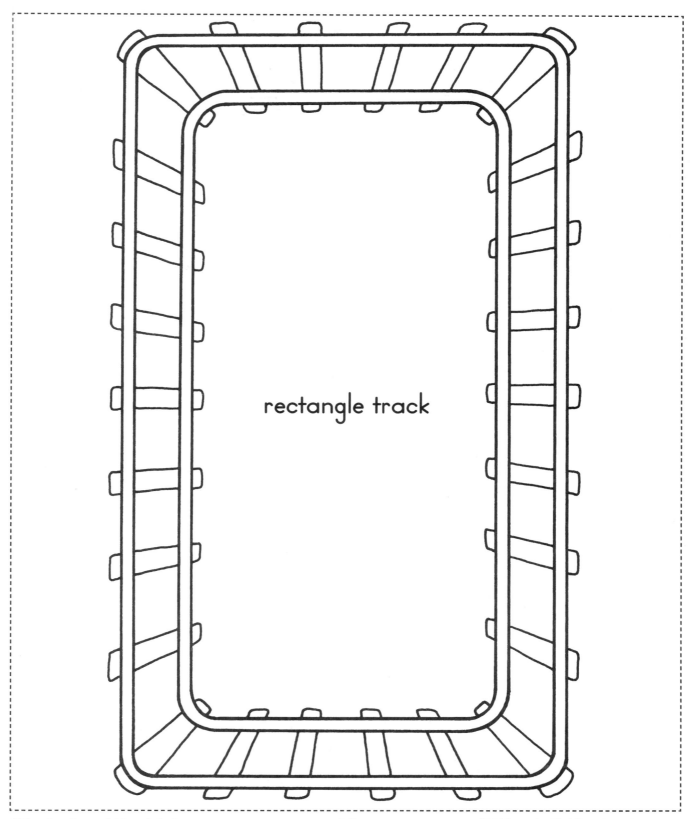

rectangle track

Trace the Track *(cont.)*

Fly Away Numbers

Skill: Sequencing numbers

Materials: scissors; butterflies (pages 152–153); wings (page 154); pencil

Teacher Preparation: Cut out butterflies and wings. Color and laminate butterflies and wings, if desired. Write the missing number on the back of each butterfly for student self-checking.

Fly Away Numbers

Student Directions

1. Choose a butterfly wing.

2. Read the number and decide which number comes next.

3. Find the wing with the number that comes next. Put it on the other side to make a butterfly.

4. Find another butterfly and repeat the process until all butterflies are complete.

5. Check your work. Look on the back of each butterfly to see if the number written matches the one on the wing you have chosen.

Fly Away Numbers *(cont.)*

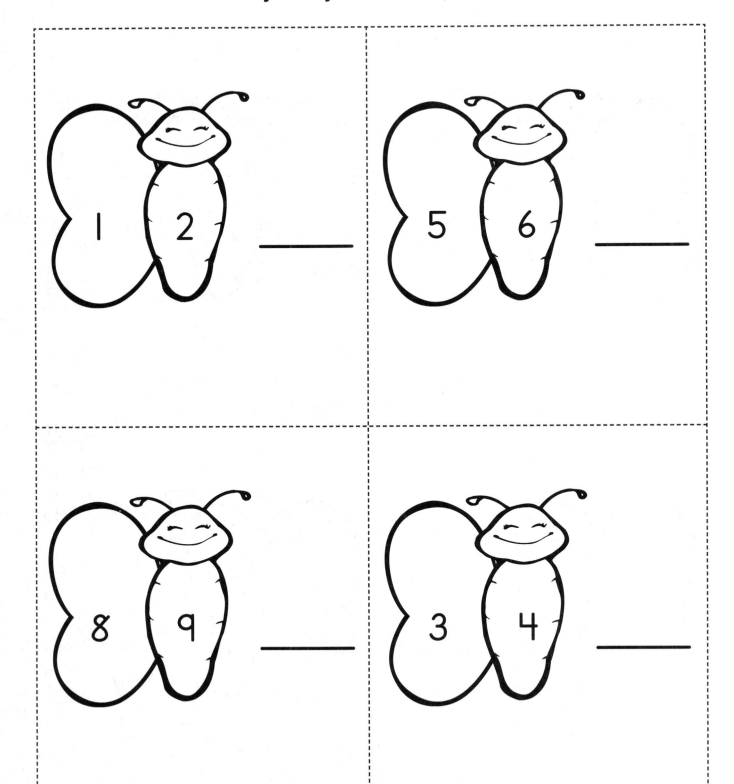

152

Fly Away Numbers *(cont.)*

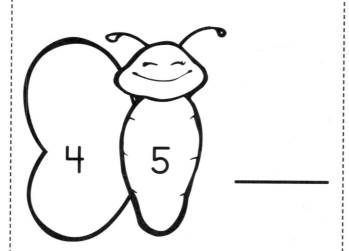 _____

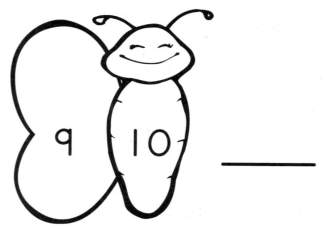 _____

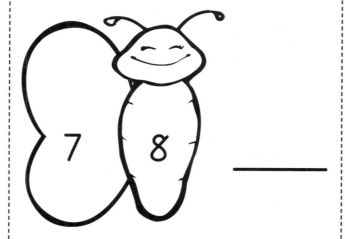 _____

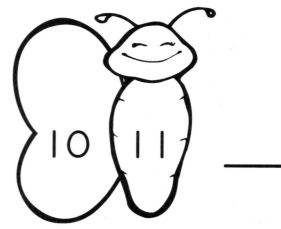 _____

Fly Away Numbers *(cont.)*

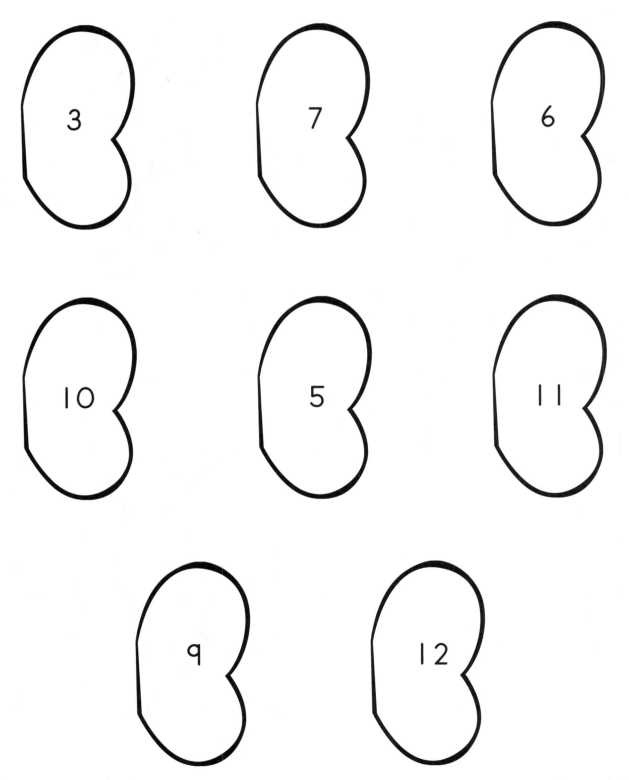

The Circle of Life

Skill: Sequencing events

Materials: scissors; life-cycle puzzle (pages 156–159); envelopes

Teacher Preparation: Cut out the life-cycle puzzles. Put each puzzle in an envelope and label it with the letter on the top of the puzzle pieces. Color and laminate puzzles, if desired.

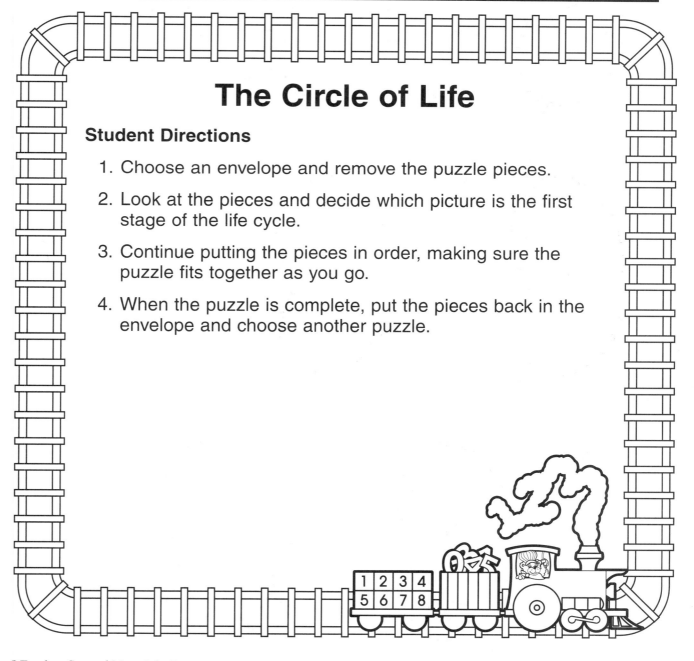

The Circle of Life

Student Directions

1. Choose an envelope and remove the puzzle pieces.

2. Look at the pieces and decide which picture is the first stage of the life cycle.

3. Continue putting the pieces in order, making sure the puzzle fits together as you go.

4. When the puzzle is complete, put the pieces back in the envelope and choose another puzzle.

The Circle of Life *(cont.)*

A

baby

A

child

A

adult

A

grandma

The Circle of Life *(cont.)*

B

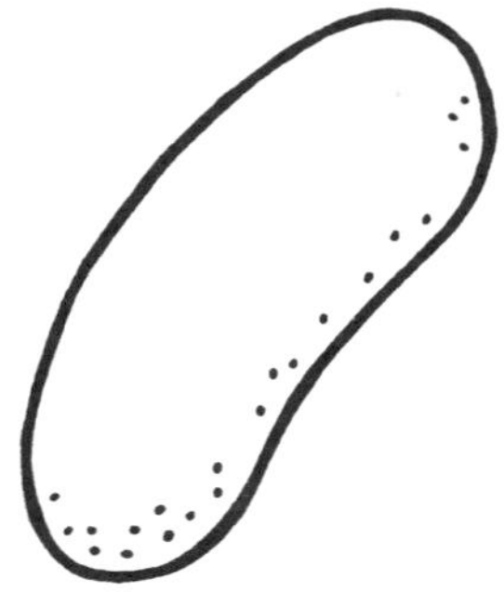

egg

B

caterpillar

B

chrysalis

B

butterfly

The Circle of Life *(cont.)*

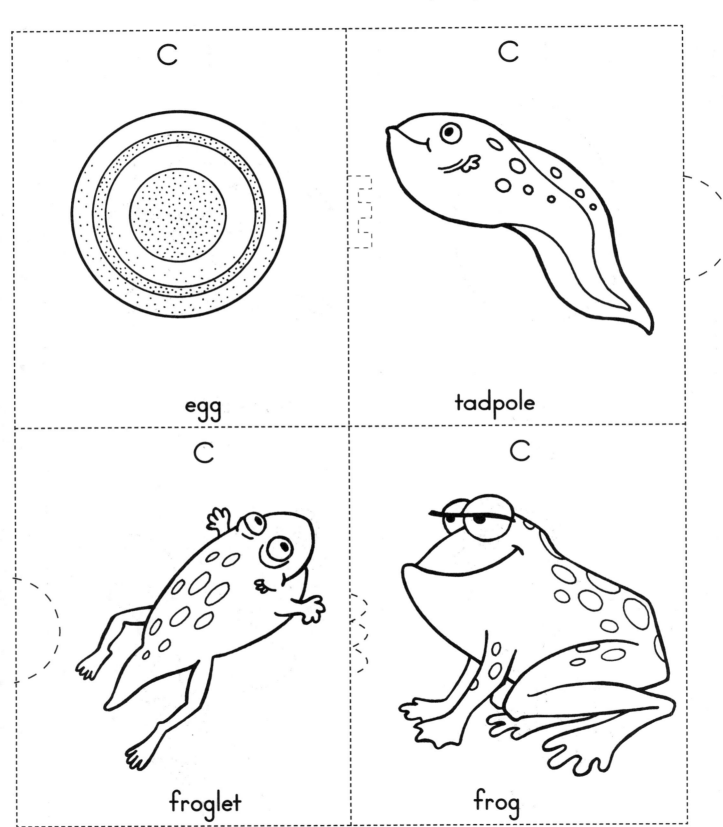

C

egg

C

tadpole

C

froglet

C

frog

The Circle of Life *(cont.)*

D

egg

D

baby chick

D

chick

D

chicken

Beach Ball Alphabet

Skill: Alphabet Sequencing

Materials: scissors; beach balls (pages 161–162); ball pieces (page 163); pencil

Teacher Preparation: Cut out beach balls and ball pieces. Color and laminate balls and ball pieces, if desired. Write the missing letter on the back of each beach ball for student self-checking.

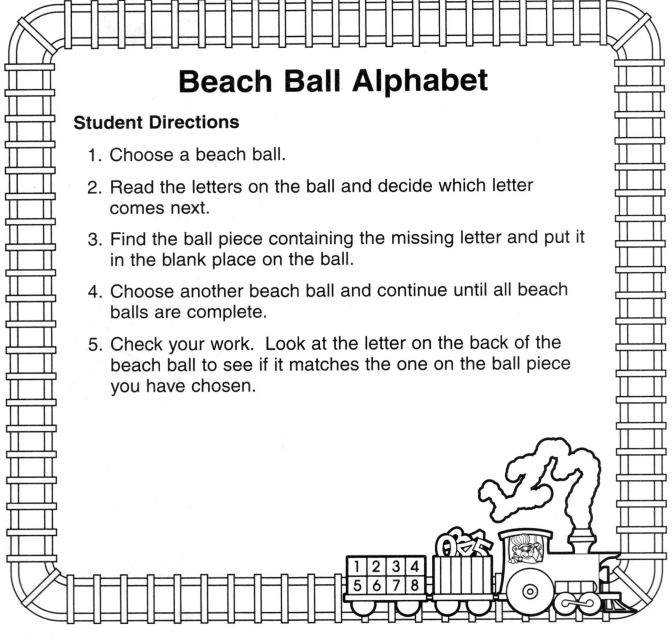

Beach Ball Alphabet

Student Directions

1. Choose a beach ball.

2. Read the letters on the ball and decide which letter comes next.

3. Find the ball piece containing the missing letter and put it in the blank place on the ball.

4. Choose another beach ball and continue until all beach balls are complete.

5. Check your work. Look at the letter on the back of the beach ball to see if it matches the one on the ball piece you have chosen.

Beach Ball Alphabet *(cont.)*

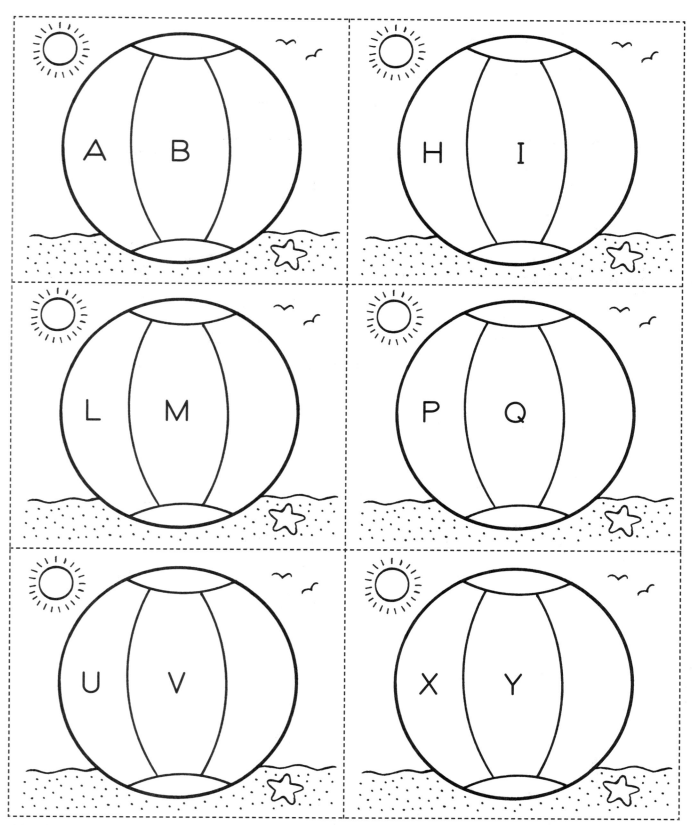

Beach Ball Alphabet *(cont.)*

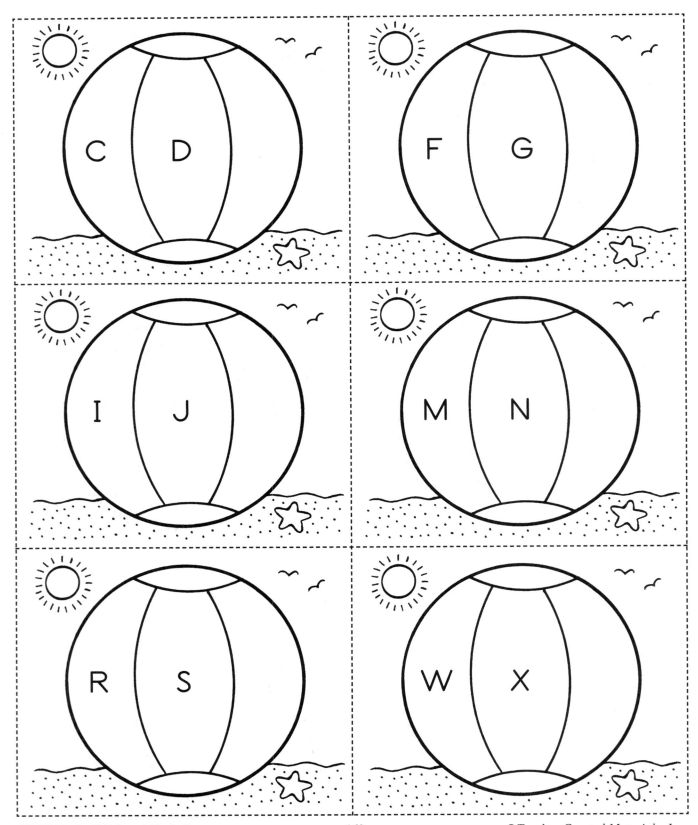

162

Beach Ball Alphabet *(cont.)*

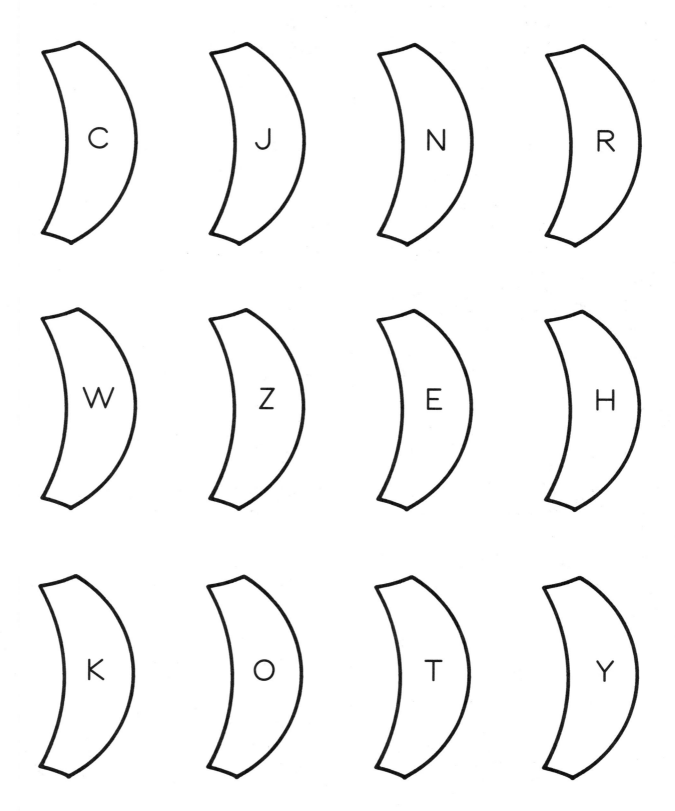

Fun with Food

Skill: Pattern Sequencing

Materials: scissors; pattern cards (pages 165–167); food cards (page 168); pencil

Teacher Preparation: Cut out food cards. Color and laminate pattern cards and food cards, if desired. Draw the missing food on the back of each pattern card for student self-checking.

Fun with Food

Student Directions

1. Choose a pattern card.
2. Say the food pattern on the first line. Decide which food comes next.
3. Find the missing food card and put it in the box next to the pattern.
4. Continue until all four patterns are complete.
5. Remove the food cards and choose another pattern card to complete.
6. Check your work. Look at the food drawn on the back of the pattern card to see if it matches the food card you have chosen.

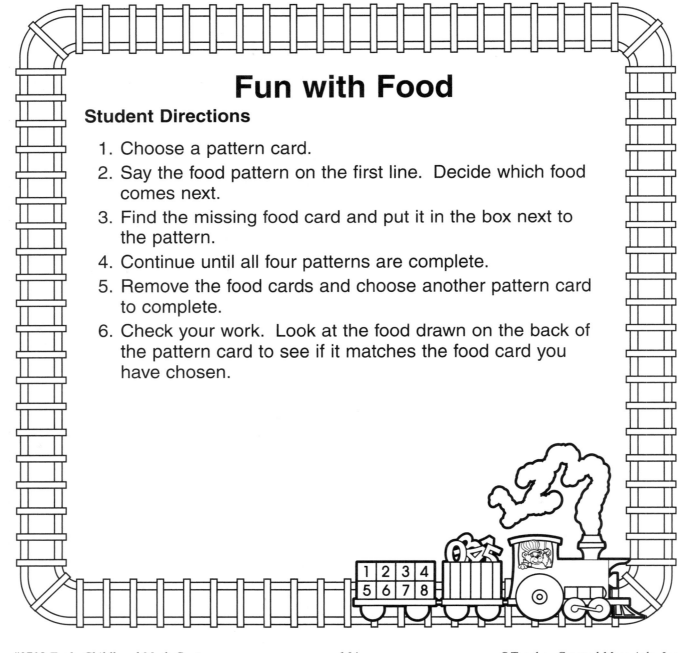

Fun With Food *(cont.)*

Fresh Food

Fun With Food *(cont.)*

Bakery

Fun With Food *(cont.)*

Hamburger Hut

Fun With Food *(cont.)*

Rhyme Time

Skill: Sequencing Events

Materials: scissors; nursery rhyme puzzles (pages 170–172); envelopes

Teacher Preparation: Cut out nursery rhyme puzzles. Put each puzzle in an envelope. Label the envelope and the back of each piece that belongs in it with the same letter for easy organization. Color and laminate puzzle pieces, if desired.

Rhyme Time

Student Directions

1. Choose an envelope and take the puzzle pieces out.

2. Determine which nursery rhyme the pictures represent and say the rhyme out loud.

3. Find the picture that comes first and place it on the table.

4. Find the next picture and fit the puzzle pieces together.

5. Continue until the puzzle is complete. Say the nursery rhyme.

6. Put the pieces back in the envelope and choose another nursery rhyme to complete.

Rhyme Time *(cont.)*

Rhyme Time *(cont.)*

Rhyme Time *(cont.)*

Easy as 1, 2, 3

Skill: Sequencing Events

Materials: scissors; sequence cards (pages 174–176); sequence mat (page 177); envelopes

Teacher Preparation: Cut out sequence cards and put them in individual envelopes. Label each envelope with the shape found at the top of the cards inside it. Color and laminate sequence cards, if desired. Number the back of each sequence card in the correct order for student self-checking.

Easy as 1, 2, 3

Student Directions

1. Put the sequence mat in front of you.
2. Choose one set of sequence cards. Place them in front of you.
3. Determine which card is first in the sequence and put it in box 1.
4. Continue the sequence with the second and third cards.
5. When the sequence is complete, check your work. Turn each card over to see if the number written on the back is the same as the number on the sequence mat.
6. Put the cards back into the envelope and choose another envelope.
7. Continue until you have completed all sequences.

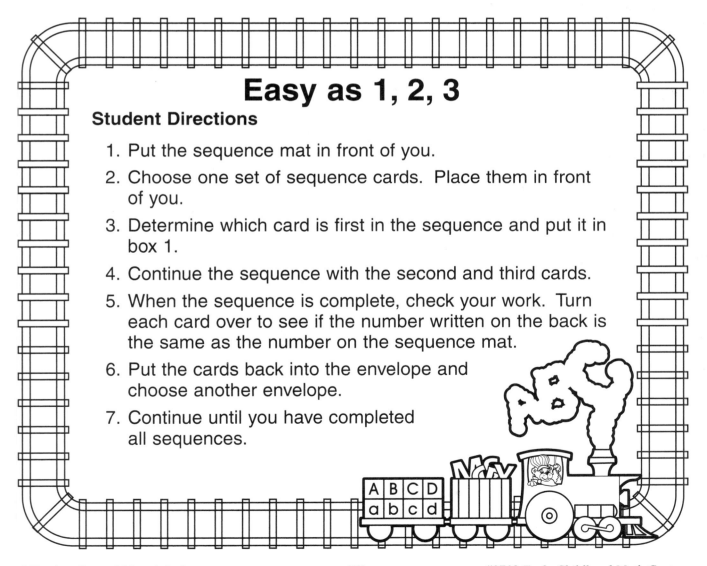

Easy as 1, 2, 3 *(cont.)*

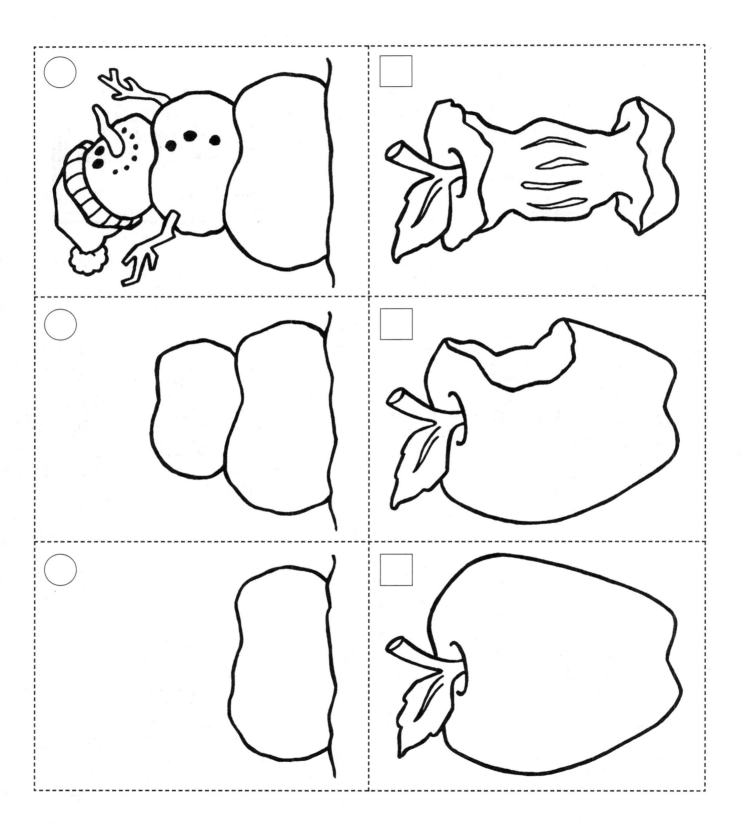

Easy as 1, 2, 3 *(cont.)*

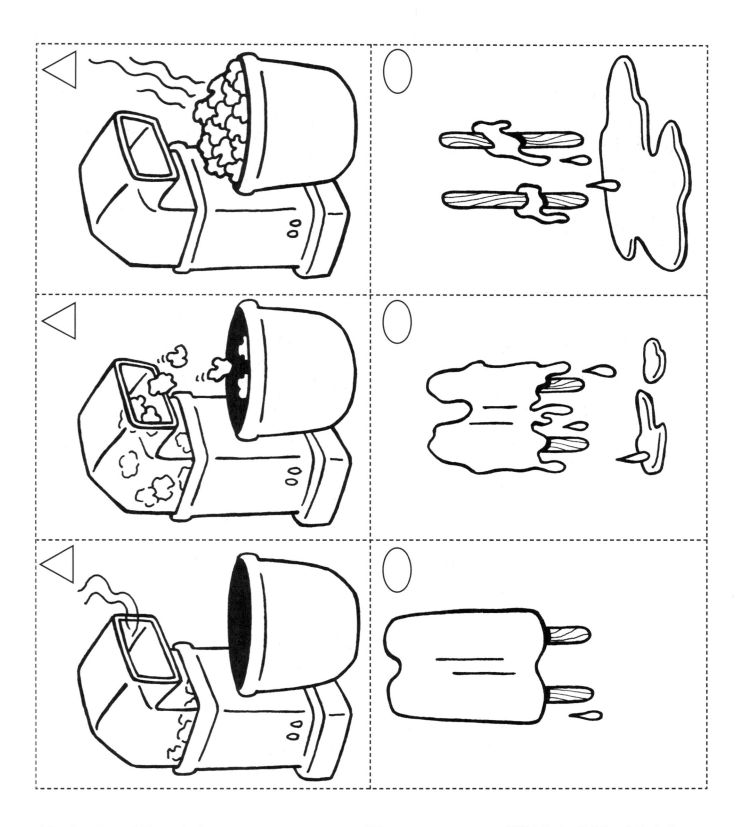

Easy as 1, 2, 3 *(cont.)*

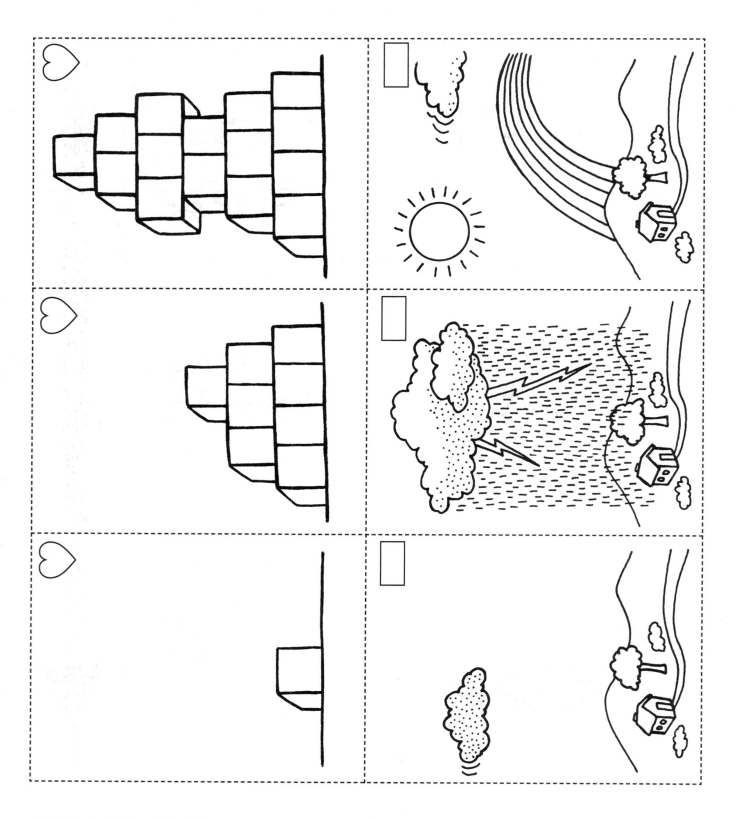

Easy as 1, 2, 3 *(cont.)*

Measure Me

Skill: Measuring

Materials: recording sheet (page 179); pictures (pages 180–183); measuring sticks (page 240); pencils or crayons

Teacher Preparation: Reproduce the recording sheet for each student. Color and laminate pictures, if desired. Assemble measuring sticks for each child in the center.

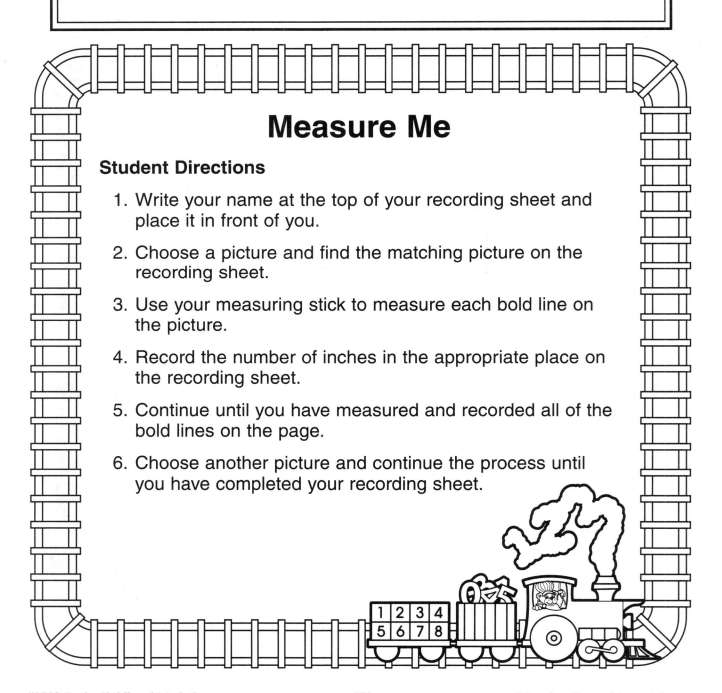

Measure Me

Student Directions

1. Write your name at the top of your recording sheet and place it in front of you.

2. Choose a picture and find the matching picture on the recording sheet.

3. Use your measuring stick to measure each bold line on the picture.

4. Record the number of inches in the appropriate place on the recording sheet.

5. Continue until you have measured and recorded all of the bold lines on the page.

6. Choose another picture and continue the process until you have completed your recording sheet.

178

Measure Me *(cont.)*

Recording Sheet   Name _____

Measure Me *(cont.)*

Lucy

180

Measure Me *(cont.)*

Jerry

Measure Me *(cont.)*

Fluffy

Measure Me *(cont.)*

Spot

Growing Garden

Skill: Measuring

Materials: scissors; stems (page 185–187); flowers (page 188); measuring sticks (page 240); pencil

Teacher Preparation: Cut out the flowers and stems. Color and laminate the flowers and stems, if desired. Write the correct number of inches on the back of each stem for student self-checking. Assemble measuring sticks.

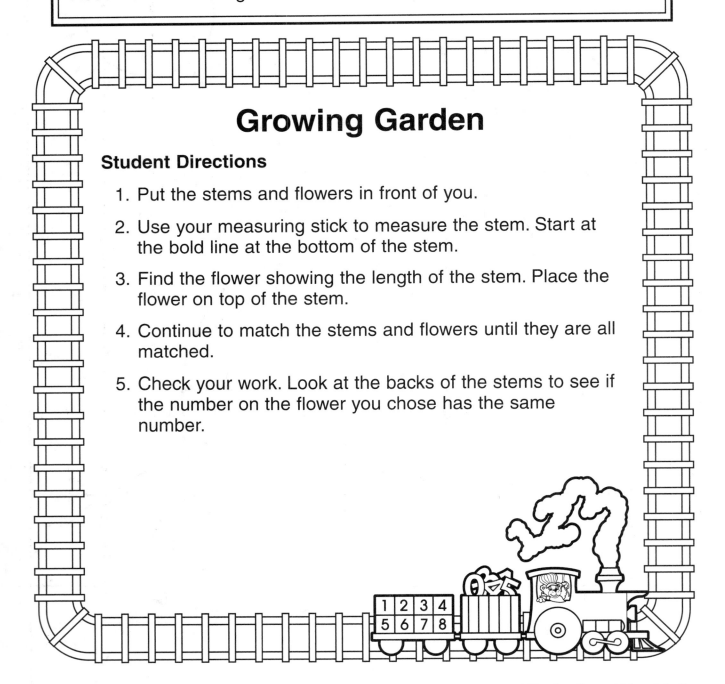

Growing Garden

Student Directions

1. Put the stems and flowers in front of you.

2. Use your measuring stick to measure the stem. Start at the bold line at the bottom of the stem.

3. Find the flower showing the length of the stem. Place the flower on top of the stem.

4. Continue to match the stems and flowers until they are all matched.

5. Check your work. Look at the backs of the stems to see if the number on the flower you chose has the same number.

Growing Garden *(cont.)*

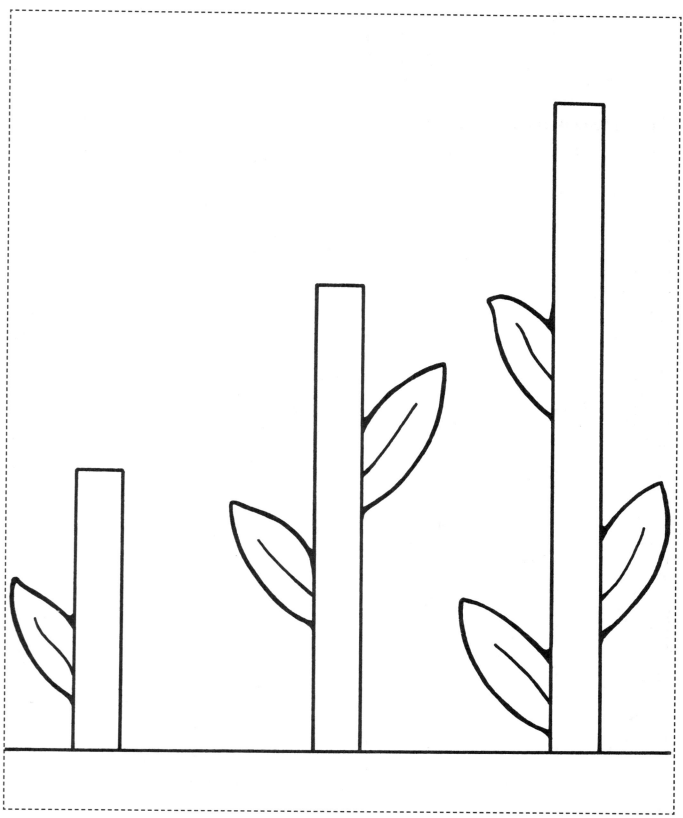

Growing Garden *(cont.)*

Growing Garden *(cont.)*

Growing Garden *(cont.)*

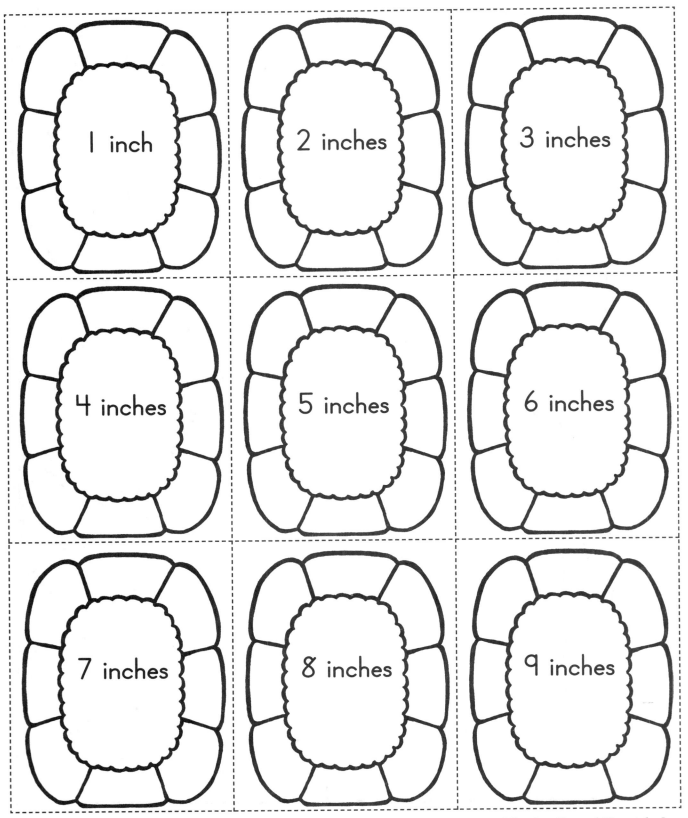

Inch Worms

Skill: Measuring, Estimating Sizes

Materials: scissors; worms (page 190); measuring cards (pages 191–193); recording sheet (page 194); pencils or crayons

Teacher Preparation: Reproduce the recording sheet for each student. Color and laminate worms and measuring cards, if desired. Cut worms and measuring cards apart on the dotted lines.

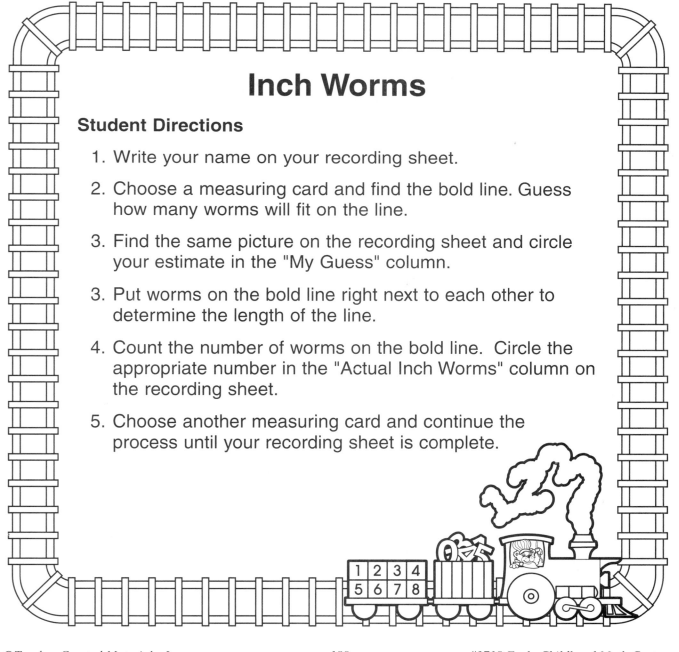

Inch Worms

Student Directions

1. Write your name on your recording sheet.

2. Choose a measuring card and find the bold line. Guess how many worms will fit on the line.

3. Find the same picture on the recording sheet and circle your estimate in the "My Guess" column.

3. Put worms on the bold line right next to each other to determine the length of the line.

4. Count the number of worms on the bold line. Circle the appropriate number in the "Actual Inch Worms" column on the recording sheet.

5. Choose another measuring card and continue the process until your recording sheet is complete.

Inch Worms *(cont.)*

190

Inch Worms *(cont.)*

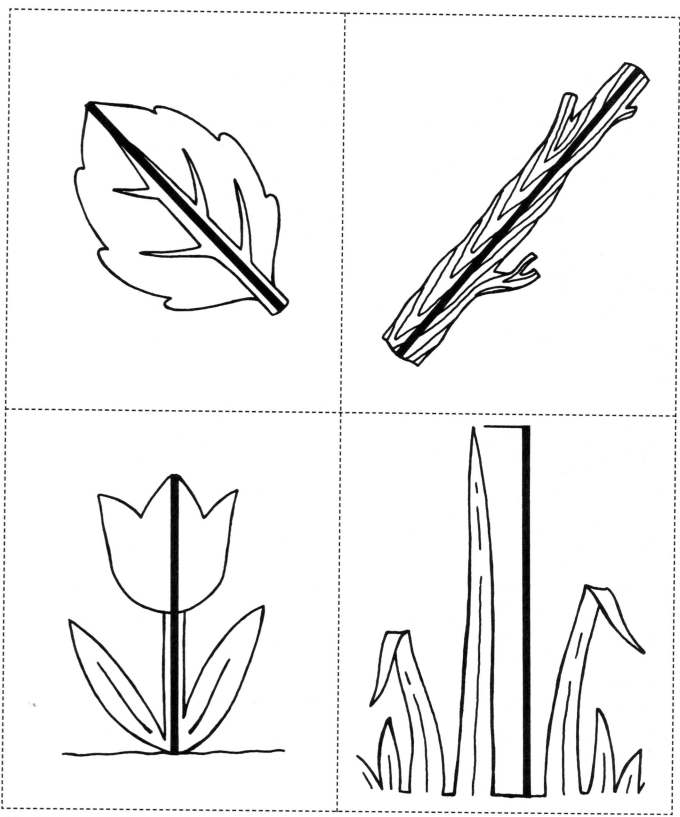

Inch Worms (cont.)

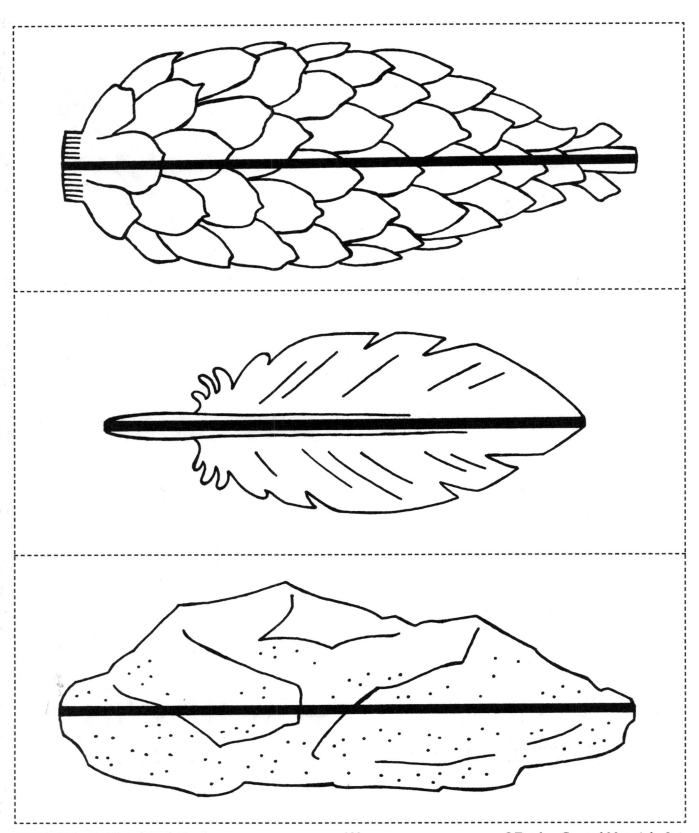

192

Inch Worms *(cont.)*

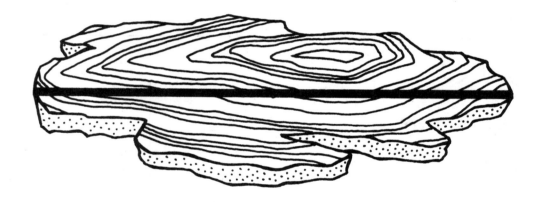

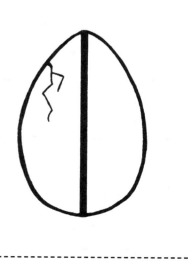

Inch Worms *(cont.)*

Name _____

Recording Sheet

Object Measured	My Guess	Actual Inch Worms
	1 2 3 4 5 6	1 2 3 4 5 6
	1 2 3 4 5 6	1 2 3 4 5 6
	1 2 3 4 5 6	1 2 3 4 5 6
	1 2 3 4 5 6	1 2 3 4 5 6
	1 2 3 4 5 6	1 2 3 4 5 6
	1 2 3 4 5 6	1 2 3 4 5 6
	1 2 3 4 5 6	1 2 3 4 5 6
	1 2 3 4 5 6	1 2 3 4 5 6
	1 2 3 4 5 6	1 2 3 4 5 6
	1 2 3 4 5 6	1 2 3 4 5 6
	1 2 3 4 5 6	1 2 3 4 5 6
	1 2 3 4 5 6	1 2 3 4 5 6

Three Bears Math

Skill: Comparing Sizes

Materials: scissors; bears (page 196); bears' belongings (pages 196 and 197); bear mats (pages 198–200); graph (page 201); pencil

Teacher Preparation: Cut out the bears, bear mats, and bear belongings. Color and laminate bears, bears' belongings, and bear mats, if desired. On the back of each of the belongings, write the name of the corresponding bear for student self-checking.

Three Bears Math

Student Directions

1. Place the three bear mats and bears in front of you.

2. Choose a bear belonging and use the bears to determine who it belongs to by matching their sizes.

3. Put it on the appropriate bear's mat.

4. Continue until you have put all the bears' belongings on the appropriate mat.

5. Check your work. Look at the back of each belonging to see if the name written on it matches the name on the mat you chose.

6. Use the graph to mark how many belongings each bear has.

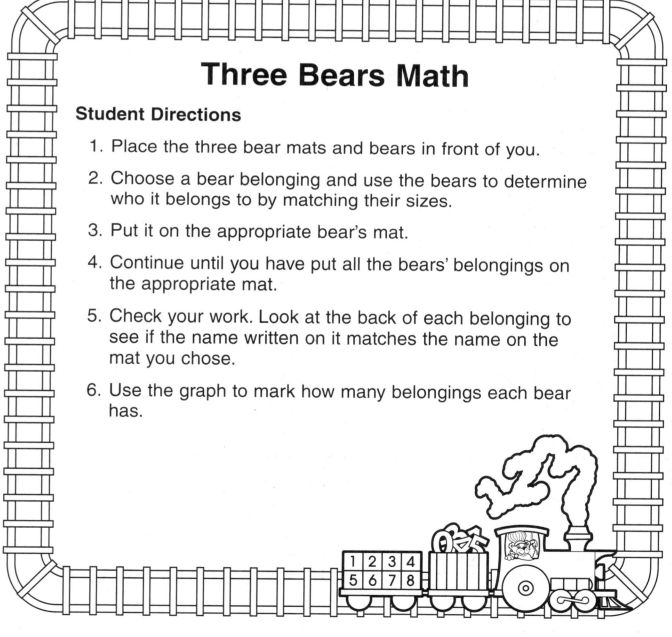

Three Bears Math *(cont.)*

Three Bears Math *(cont.)*

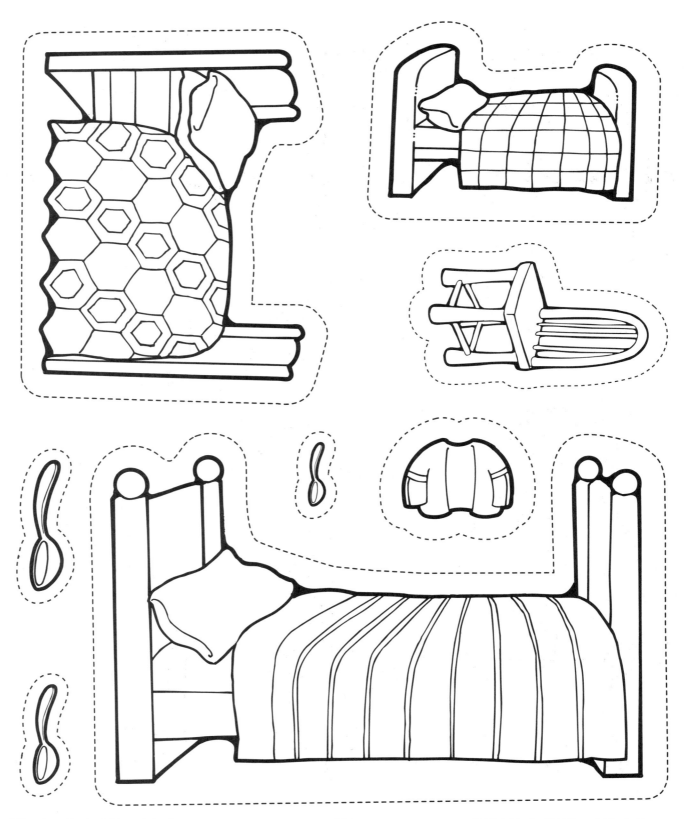

Three Bears Math *(cont.)*

Three Bears Math *(cont.)*

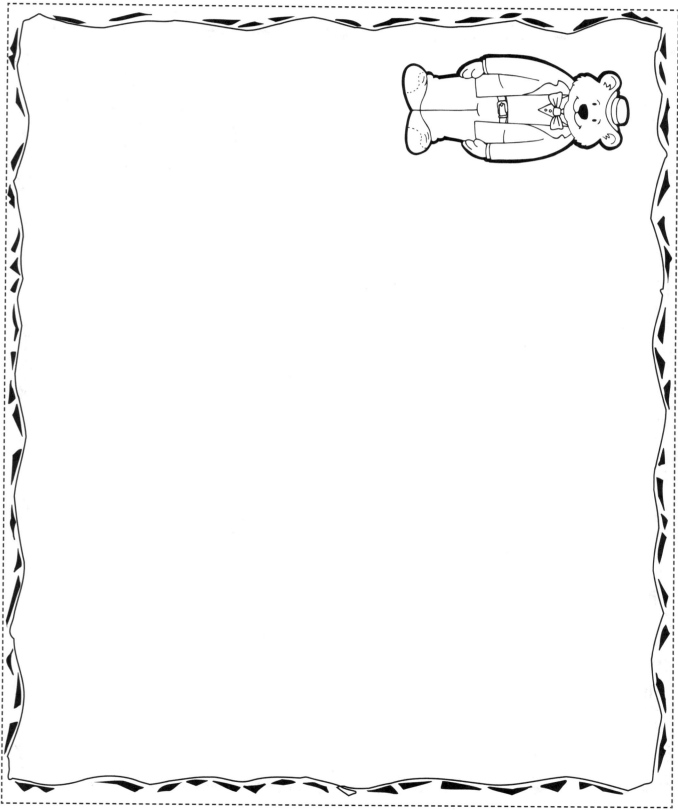

Three Bears Math *(cont.)*

Three Bears Math *(cont.)*

My Graph

Name _____

8			
7			
6			
5			
4			
3			
2			
1			

Hair Cut

Skill: Measuring

Materials: hair reproducible (page 203); scissors; measurement cards (page 204); recording sheet (page 205); scissors; glue

Teacher Preparation: Reproduce hair and recording sheets for each student. Cut measurement cards on the dotted lines. Laminate the measurement cards if possible.

Hair Cut

Student Directions

1. Write your name on your recording sheet.

2. Cut hair pictures on the dotted lines to make four heads of hair.

3. Choose a measurement card. Place it on top of one of the heads of hair.

4. Match up the bold line and star at the top of the hair and measurement card.

5. Carefully cut the hair just below the measurement card. Be very careful not to cut the measurement card.

6. Determine the length of the hair by the number on the measurement card. Glue the hair on the appropriate box on the recording sheet.

7. Continue until your recording sheet is full.

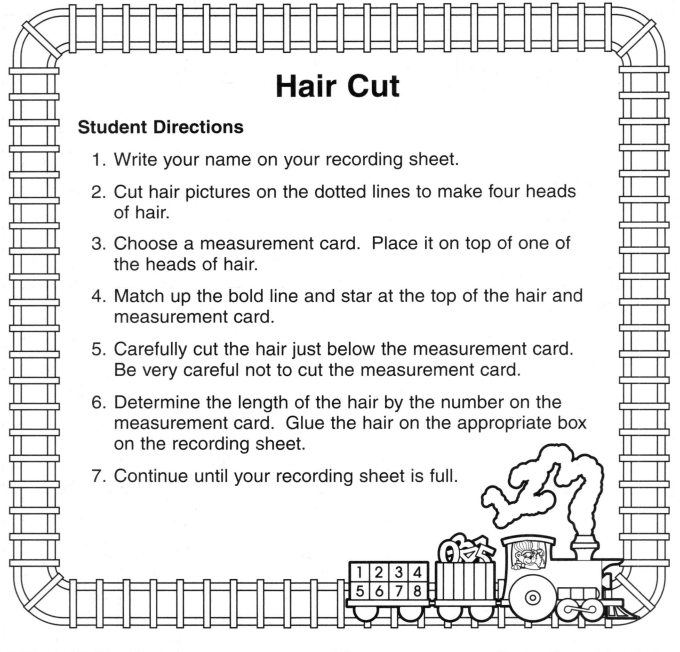

Hair Cut (cont.)

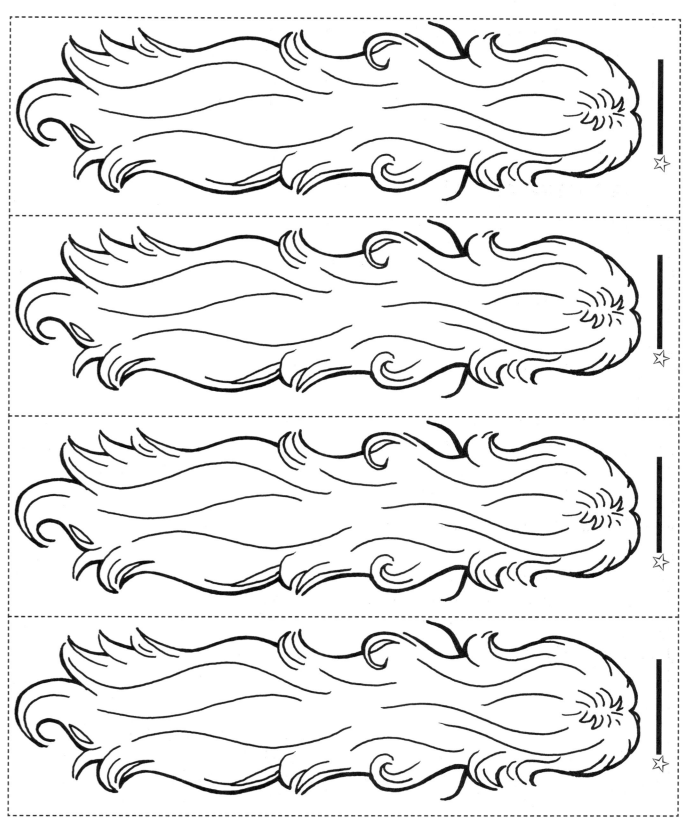

Hair Cut *(cont.)*

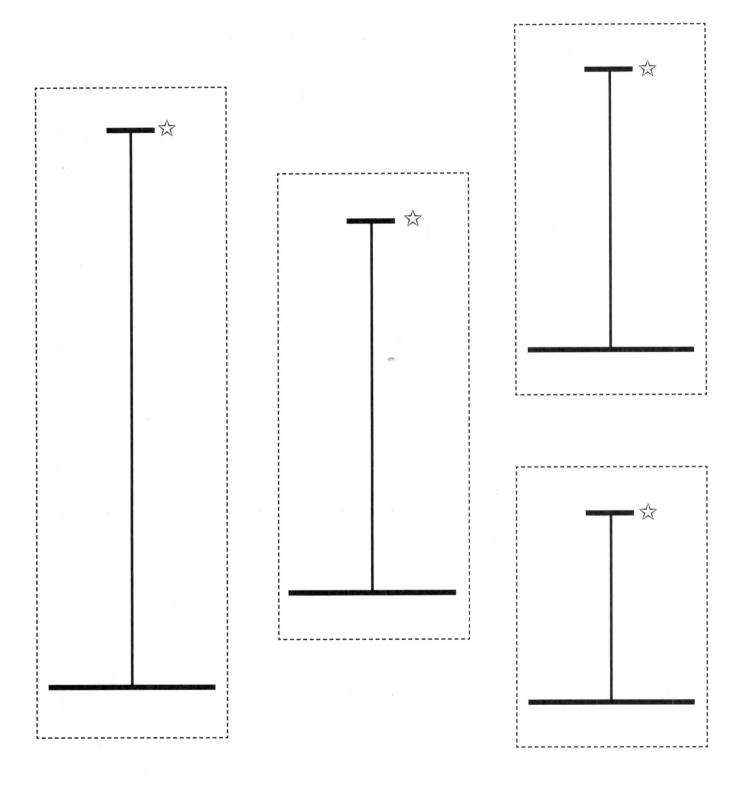

204

Hair Cut *(cont.)*

Name _____

2 inches

3 inches

4 inches

6 inches

Big Fruit, Little Fruit

Skill: Measuring, Comparing Sizes

Materials: mini-books (pages 207–209); fruit (page 210); pencils or crayons; scissors; glue

Teacher Preparation: Reproduce and assemble a mini book for each student. Reproduce fruit for each student.

Big Fruit, Little Fruit

Student Directions

1. Write your name on the cover of the mini book.

2. Cut out fruit on the dotted lines. Place them in front of you.

3. Look at the first page of the mini book and find the one-inch line.

4. Find two pieces of fruit that are one-inch long by measuring them on the bold lines on the fruit. When you find the fruits that are the same length as the lines, glue them on the lines.

5. Continue until all of the fruit is glued in the mini book.

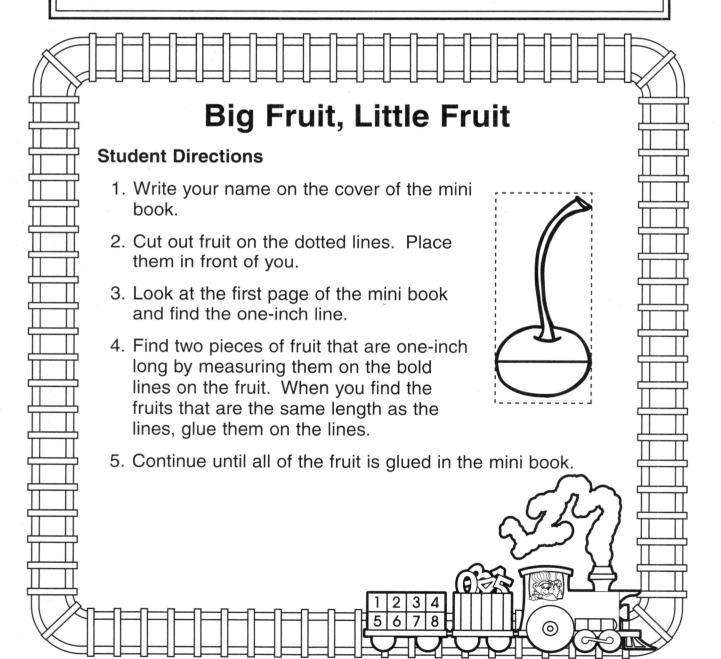

Big Fruit, Little Fruit *(cont.)*

Big Fruit, Little Fruit

By: _____

This is 1 inch: ├─────────┤. Find **2** pieces of fruit that are 1 inch long and glue them to this page.

├─────────┤   ├─────────┤

1 inch   1 inch

1

Big Fruit, Little Fruit *(cont.)*

This is 2 inches: |————————————| . Find 2 pieces of fruit that are 2 inches long and glue them to this page.

|————————————|
2 inches

|————————————|
2 inches

2

This is 3 inches: |————————————————|. Find 2 pieces of fruit that are 3 inches long and glue them to this page.

|————————————|
3 inches

|————————————|
3 inches

3

Measurement

Big Fruit, Little Fruit *(cont.)*

This is 4 inches: ⊢————————————⊣.
Find a piece of fruit that is 4 inches long and glue it to this page.

⊢————————————⊣

4 inches

4

This is 5 inches: ⊢————————————⊣.
Find a piece of fruit that is 5 inches long and glue it to this page.

⊢————————————⊣

5 inches

5

Big Fruit, Little Fruit *(cont.)*

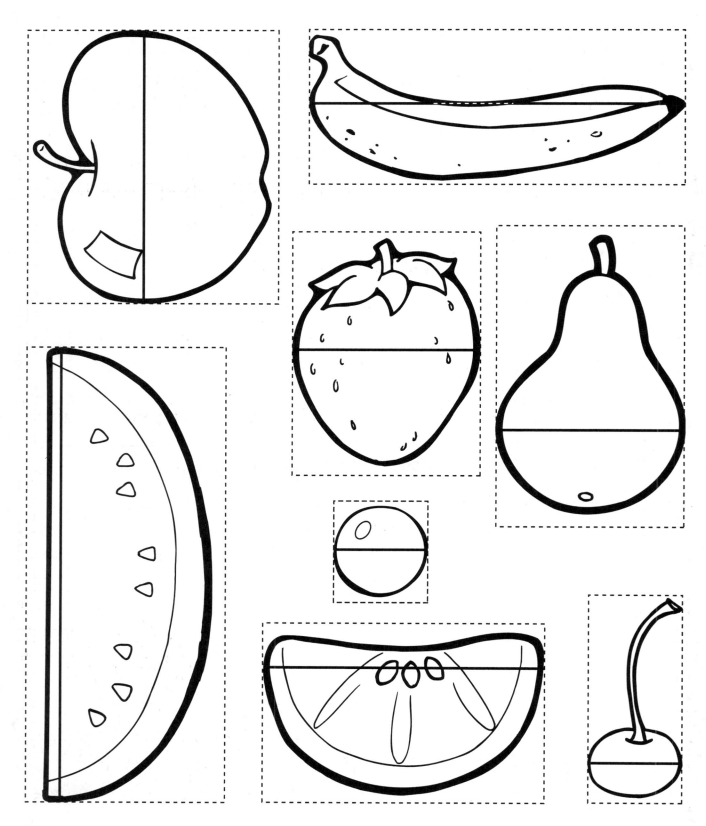

Create a Graph

Skill: Creating Graphs from Data

Materials: scissors; color cards (pages 212–213); graph (page 214); helping page (page 215); one die; pencils or crayons

Teacher Preparation: Reproduce one graph for each student. Color the color cards and helping page. Cut out color cards. Laminate the color cards and helping page, if desired.

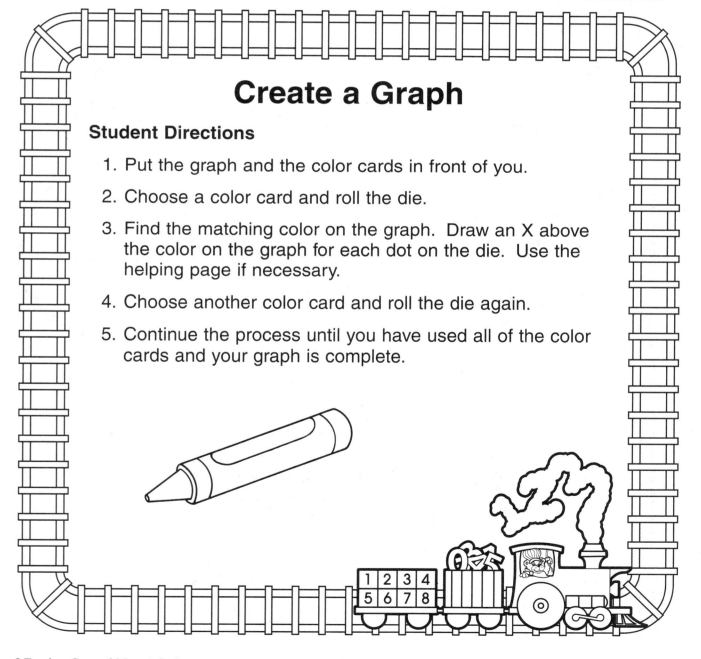

Create a Graph

Student Directions

1. Put the graph and the color cards in front of you.

2. Choose a color card and roll the die.

3. Find the matching color on the graph. Draw an X above the color on the graph for each dot on the die. Use the helping page if necessary.

4. Choose another color card and roll the die again.

5. Continue the process until you have used all of the color cards and your graph is complete.

Create a Graph *(cont.)*

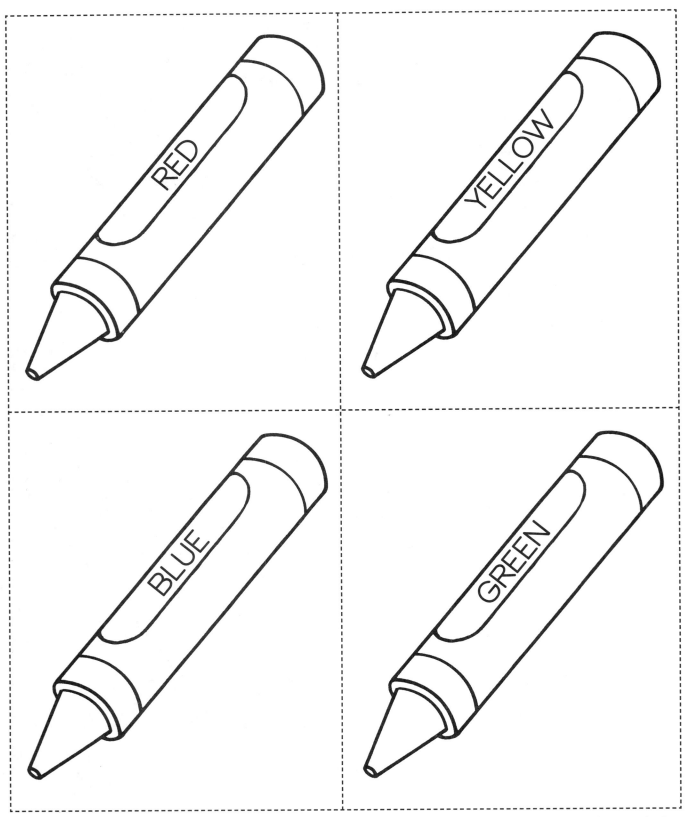

Create a Graph *(cont.)*

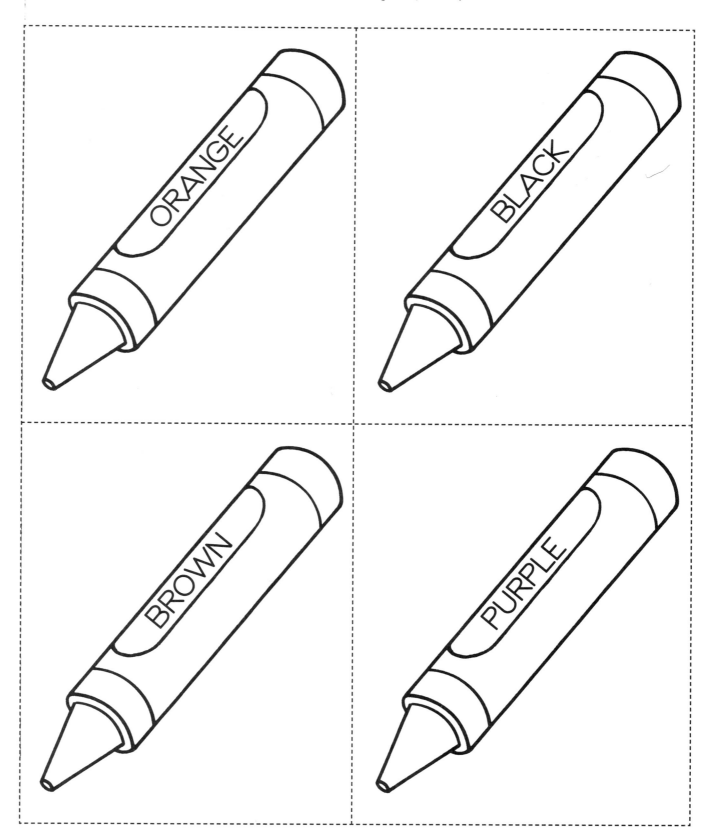

#3718 Early Childhood Math Centers

Create a Graph *(cont.)*

Name _____

	1	2	3	4	5	6
RED						
BLUE						
YELLOW						
GREEN						
ORANGE						
BROWN						
BLACK						
PURPLE						

Create a Graph *(cont.)*

COLOR WORDS

HELPING PAGE

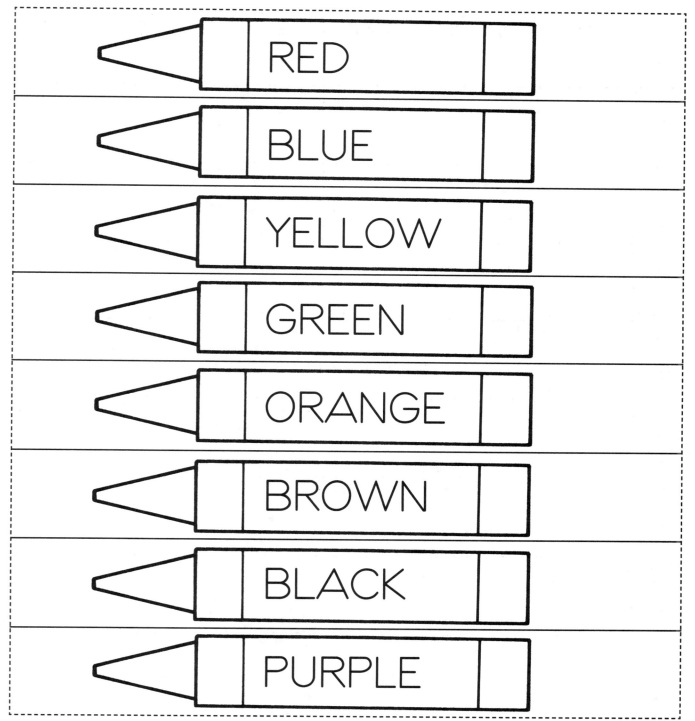

RED

BLUE

YELLOW

GREEN

ORANGE

BROWN

BLACK

PURPLE

My Graph

Skill: Creating Graphs from Data

Materials: mini-books (pages 217–219); graph (page 220); pencils or crayons

Teacher Preparation: Reproduce and assemble one mini book for each student using the mini-book pages. Reproduce one graph for each student. Students will need instruction on how to complete the mini book and graph prior to going to the center.

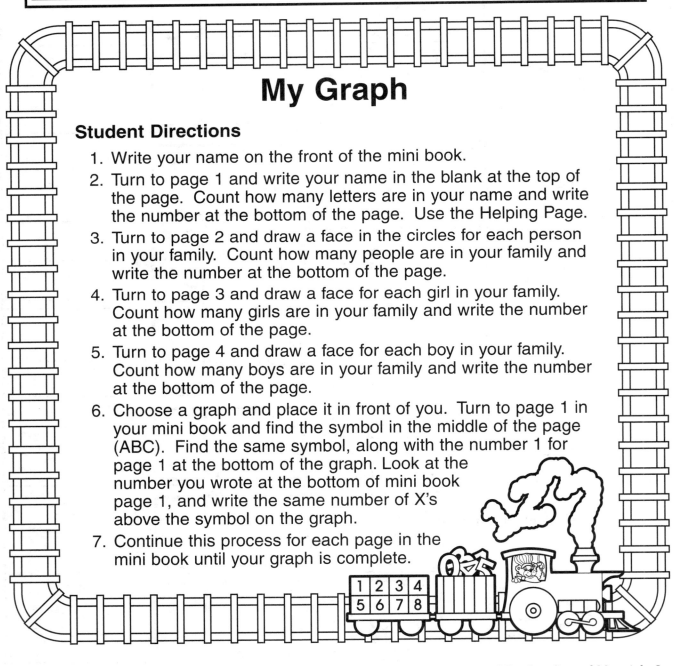

My Graph

Student Directions

1. Write your name on the front of the mini book.

2. Turn to page 1 and write your name in the blank at the top of the page. Count how many letters are in your name and write the number at the bottom of the page. Use the Helping Page.

3. Turn to page 2 and draw a face in the circles for each person in your family. Count how many people are in your family and write the number at the bottom of the page.

4. Turn to page 3 and draw a face for each girl in your family. Count how many girls are in your family and write the number at the bottom of the page.

5. Turn to page 4 and draw a face for each boy in your family. Count how many boys are in your family and write the number at the bottom of the page.

6. Choose a graph and place it in front of you. Turn to page 1 in your mini book and find the symbol in the middle of the page (ABC). Find the same symbol, along with the number 1 for page 1 at the bottom of the graph. Look at the number you wrote at the bottom of mini book page 1, and write the same number of X's above the symbol on the graph.

7. Continue this process for each page in the mini book until your graph is complete.

My Graph *(cont.)*

All About Me

By: _____

My name is _____

How many letters $\boxed{\begin{array}{l} A \\ B \\ C \end{array}}$ in your name?

_____

①

My Graph *(cont.)*

Draw a face for each person in your family.

How many people  in your family?

_____

②

Draw a face for each girl in your family.

How many girls  in your family?

_____

③

My Graph *(cont.)*

Draw a face for each boy in your family.

How many boys  in your family?

_____

Helping Page

1 ○	5 ○ ○ ○ ○ ○	
2 ○ ○	6 ○ ○ ○ ○ ○ ○	
3 ○ ○ ○	7 ○ ○ ○ ○ ○ ○ ○	
4 ○ ○ ○ ○	8 ○ ○ ○ ○ ○ ○ ○ ○	

My Graph *(cont.)*

My Graph

Name ______________________________

8				
7				
6				
5				
4				
3				
2				
1				
	How many letters A B C in your name? (1)	How many people 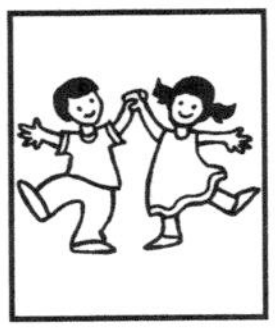 in your family? (2)	How many girls 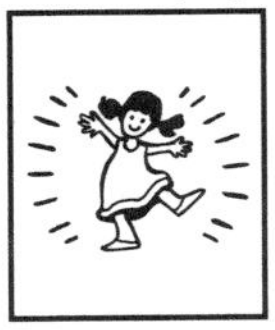 in your family? (3)	How many boys 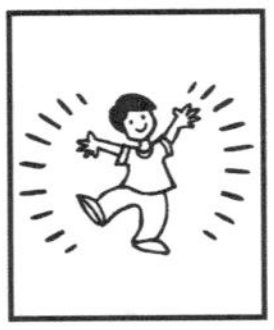 in your family? (4)

Critter Count

Skill: Creating Graphs From Data

Materials: animal sheets (pages 222–223); graphs (pages 224–225); crayons or pencils

Teacher Preparation: Reproduce graphs for each student in your class. Color and laminate animal sheets, if desired.

Critter Count

Student Directions

1. Choose a graph and find the letter in the top right corner. Find the animal sheet with the same letter in the top right corner.

2. Look at the first animal on the page and count how many there are.

3. Find the animal on the graph and write an X on the graph above its picture for each animal you counted.

4. Continue until you have completed the graph.

5. Choose another graph and matching animal page to complete.

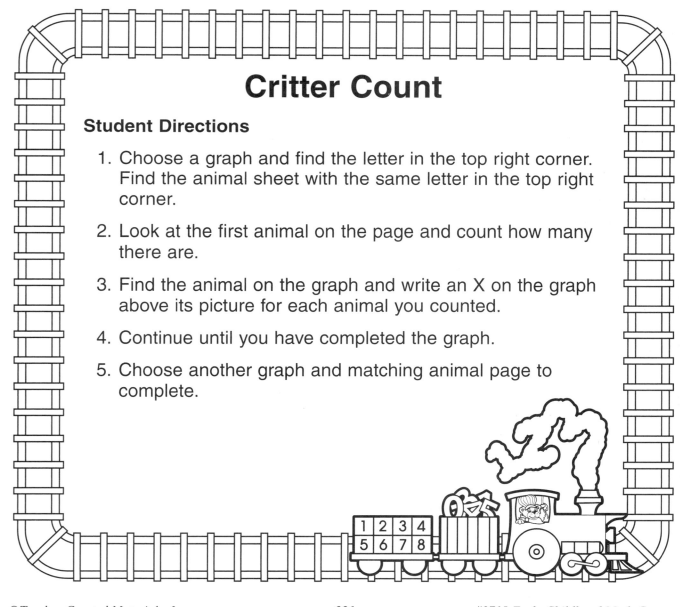

Critter Count *(cont.)*

a

fish	
lobster	
octopus	
clam	
whale	
shark	

Critter Count *(cont.)*

b

elephant	
zebra	
monkey	
giraffe	
hippo	
bear	

Critters Count (cont.)

a

	fish	lobster	octopus	clam	whale	shark
6						
5						
4						
3						
2						
1						

Critters Count *(cont.)*

b

6						
5						
4						
3						
2						
1						
	monkey	bear	zebra	giraffe	elephant	hippo

Count on Me

Skill: Interpreting Data from Graphs

Materials: scissors; graphs (pages 227–230); number cards (page 231); envelopes

Teacher Preparation: Cut out number cards. Laminate graphs and number cards, if desired. Attach an envelope to the back of each graph and put a set of number cards in it.

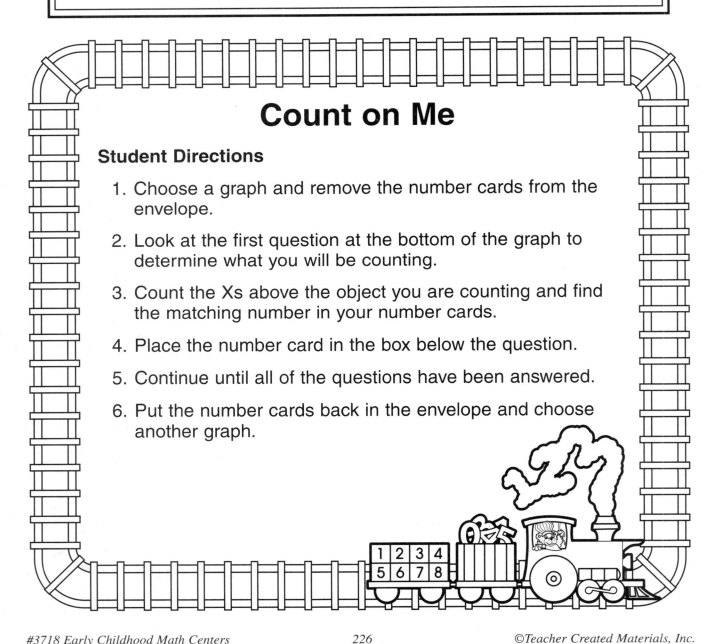

Count on Me

Student Directions

1. Choose a graph and remove the number cards from the envelope.

2. Look at the first question at the bottom of the graph to determine what you will be counting.

3. Count the Xs above the object you are counting and find the matching number in your number cards.

4. Place the number card in the box below the question.

5. Continue until all of the questions have been answered.

6. Put the number cards back in the envelope and choose another graph.

Count on Me *(cont.)*

5			X	
4			X	X
3		X	X	X
2	X	X	X	X
1	X	X	X	X
	△	♡	○	□

How many ♡?　How many ○ ?　How many △ ?　How many □ ?

Count on Me *(cont.)*

5				X
4			X	X
3	X		X	X
2	X		X	X
1	X	X	X	X
	skate	skis	sled	snowman

How many skate ? How many skis ? How many sled ? How many snowman ?

Count on Me *(cont.)*

5	X			
4	X			
3	X	X		
2	X	X		
1	X	X	X	
				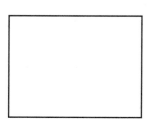

How many ?   How many ?   How many ?   How many ?

         #3718 Early Childhood Math Centers

Count on Me *(cont.)*

5		X		
4	X	X		
3	X	X		
2	X	X	X	
1	X	X	X	X
				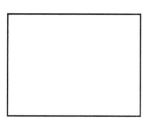

How many ?   How many ?   How many ?   How many ?

Count on Me *(cont.)*

1	1	1	1
2	2	2	2
3	3	3	3
4	4	4	4
5	5	5	5

Pie Graph

Skill: Creating Graphs from Data, Pie Graphs

Materials: scissors; pie orders (page 233); recording sheet (page 234); crayons (red, yellow, orange and blue); helping page (page 235)

Teacher Preparation: Cut apart the pie orders. Reproduce the recording page for each student. Color fruit pictures on the pie orders and helping page as indicated on the helping page. Laminate the helping page and pie orders, if desired.

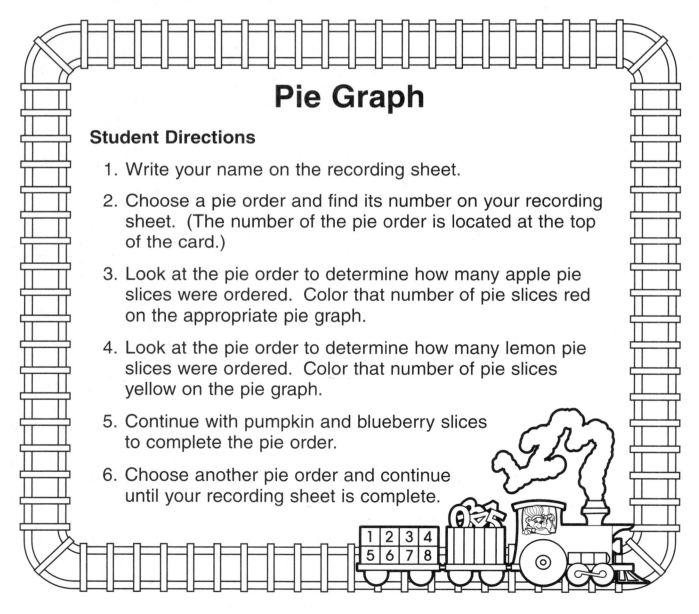

Pie Graph

Student Directions

1. Write your name on the recording sheet.

2. Choose a pie order and find its number on your recording sheet. (The number of the pie order is located at the top of the card.)

3. Look at the pie order to determine how many apple pie slices were ordered. Color that number of pie slices red on the appropriate pie graph.

4. Look at the pie order to determine how many lemon pie slices were ordered. Color that number of pie slices yellow on the pie graph.

5. Continue with pumpkin and blueberry slices to complete the pie order.

6. Choose another pie order and continue until your recording sheet is complete.

| 1 | 2 | 3 | 4 |
| 5 | 6 | 7 | 8 |

232

Pie Graph *(cont.)*

Pie Order #1			Pie Order #2		
🍎	2	● ●	🍎	1	●
🍋	2	● ●	🍋	2	● ●
🎃	2	● ●	🎃	3	● ● ●
🫐	2	● ●	🫐	2	● ●
Pie Order #3			Pie Order #4		
🍎	2	● ●	🍎	1	●
🍋	4	● ● ● ●	🍋	2	● ●
🎃	1	●	🎃	0	
🫐	1	●	🫐	5	● ● ● ● ●

Pie Graph *(cont.)*

Recording Sheet and Key   Name: _____

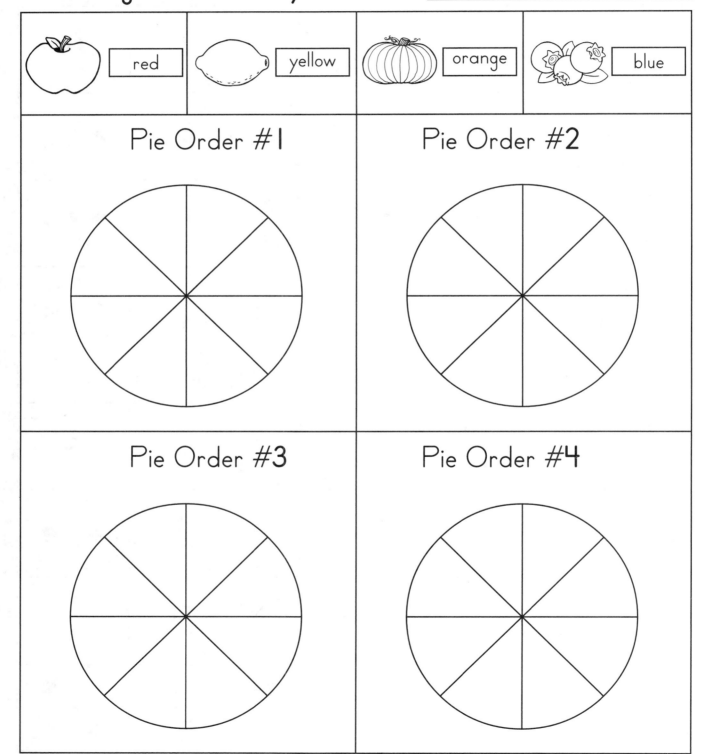

| apple | red | lemon | yellow | pumpkin | orange | blueberries | blue |

Pie Order #1   Pie Order #2

Pie Order #3   Pie Order #4

Pie Graph *(cont.)*

Helping Page

red

yellow

orange

blue

Pet Parade

Skill: Creating Graphs from Data

Materials: pets (page 237); graph (page 238); number helping page (page 239); one die; tape; pencils or crayons

Teacher Preparation: Reproduce a pet page and graph for each student.

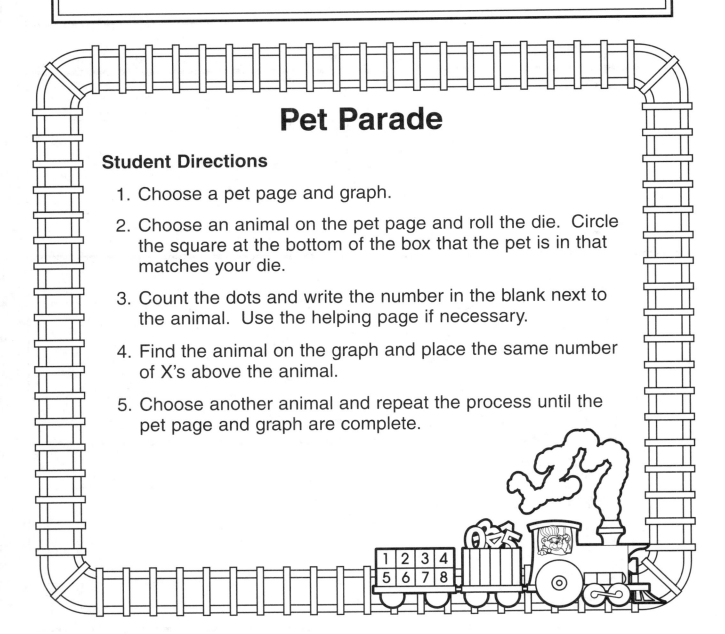

Pet Parade

Student Directions

1. Choose a pet page and graph.

2. Choose an animal on the pet page and roll the die. Circle the square at the bottom of the box that the pet is in that matches your die.

3. Count the dots and write the number in the blank next to the animal. Use the helping page if necessary.

4. Find the animal on the graph and place the same number of X's above the animal.

5. Choose another animal and repeat the process until the pet page and graph are complete.

Pet Parade *(cont.)*

Pet Parade *(cont.)*

6						
5						
4						
3						
2						
1						
	dog	cat	fish	snake	frog	gerbil

Pet Parade *(cont.)*

Number Helping Page Center

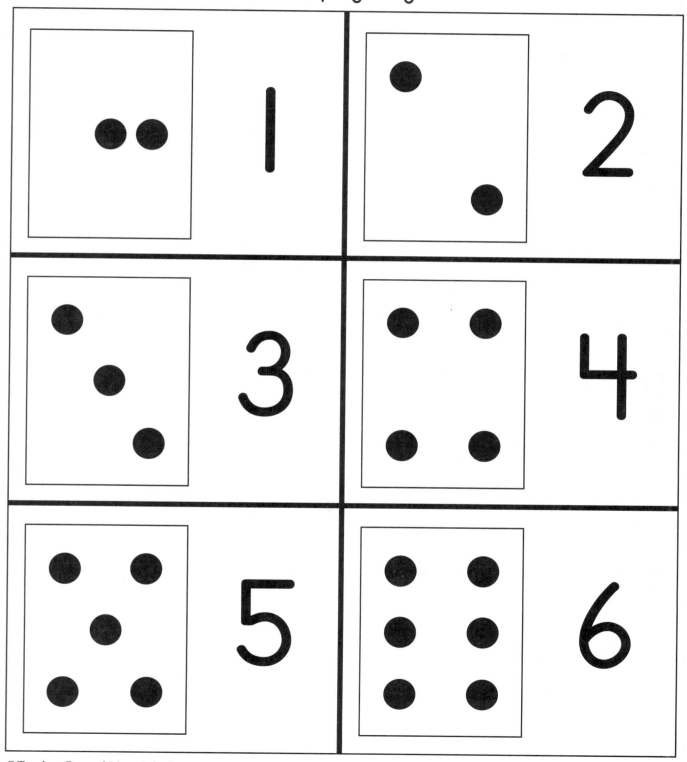

Measuring Sticks

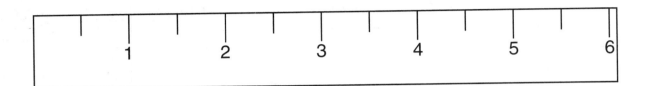

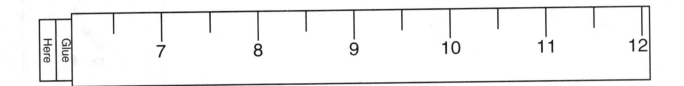

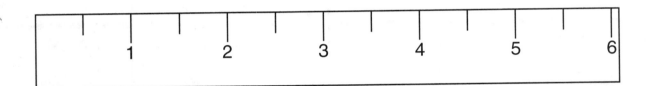

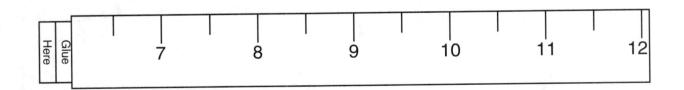

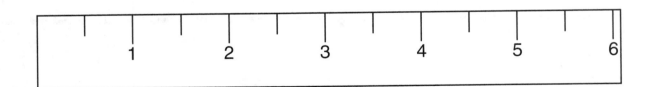

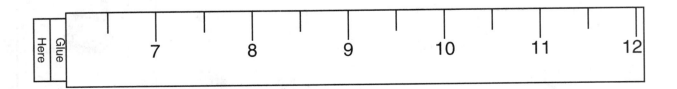